MERSEY SHIPPING MEMORIES

by

Ian Collard

INTRODUCTION

I was born and brought up in Birkenhead and in my earlier years the docks became our playground. In those days, the entire dock estate was home to different stevedoring, warehousing, packing and manufacturing firms, and the docks were always occupied by ships of every type and nationality. The Mersey was home to many of the world's largest shipping lines; regular liner and cargo services were operated from Liverpool and Birkenhead docks in the 1950s and 1960s when most of these photographs were taken. I quickly graduated from a simple box camera to a Pentax which was given to me as a birthday present. I later acquired another Pentax, using one for black & white and the other for colour slides and prints.

It is now difficult to appreciate the volume of traffic at the port in those days when you could witness four large fully-laden cargo vessels locking down in Alfred or Sandon Dock. There would be a similar number waiting in the river to dock on that tide and move to their loading berths. The main shipping lines operating from the port were Blue Funnel, Clan, Ellerman, Elder Dempster, Harrison, Anchor, Cunard, Canadian Pacific, Bibby, Brocklebank, Booth, Furness Withy, Blue Star, Lamport & Holt, Shaw Savill & Albion, Pacific Steam Navigation. Several foreign shipping companies also called regularly including Lykes Lines, Saguenay, Scindia, Safmarine and Nippon Yusen Kaisha. The images in this book concentrate on the classic cargo ships.

It was a time when people travelled by passenger liners and these regularly berthed at the landing stage at Liverpool Pier Head. Cunard and Canadian Pacific operated a passenger and cargo service across the Atlantic to Canada and the United States. Elder Dempster sailed to West Africa, and Pacific Steam Navigation sailed to South America. Bibby, Anchor and Henderson Lines also provided a passenger and cargo service to Burma, Ceylon, India and Pakistan.

The Mersey is also the main gateway to Ireland and the Isle of Man. Coastal passenger services were operated by the Belfast Steamship Company, British & Irish Steam Packet Company and Isle of Man Steam Packet Company. Coastal vessels also traded to Denmark, Holland, Germany and other European destinations.

The majority of the images in this book concentrate on classic cargo ships and were taken during this period, prior to the introduction of containerisation and the Boeing 737 which brought about the demise of the conventional cargo ship and the closure of passenger services from the Mersey. Most of the photographs have never been published before and others have been seen only as black & white images. All photographs were taken by the author except where credited otherwise.

The information in brackets after each ship's name denotes the flag of the ship when not British, gross registered tonnage and year of completion. The gross registered tonnage figures could vary during the life of the ships but those used have been taken from *Lloyd's Register*.

Acknowledgements

I wish to thank all those who have helped in any way with the production of this book. Special thanks go to those who have loaned their transparencies. I also wish to record my thanks to those who have read the first drafts of the book, especially Gil Mayes, and have suggested corrections and improvements. Thanks also must go to the Amadeus Press for bringing the book to a successful conclusion.

Ian Collard Wallasey July 2007

Published by Bernard McCall, 400 Nore Road, Portishead, Bristol, BS20 8EZ, England. Website : www.coastalshipping.co.uk
Telephone/fax : 01275 846178. E-mail : bernard@coastalshipping.co.uk
All distribution enquiries should be addressed to the publisher.

Printed by Amadeus Press, Ezra House, West 26 Business Park, Cleckheaton, West Yorkshire, BD19 4TQ
Telephone : 01274 863210; fax : 01274 863211; e-mail : info@amadeuspress.co.uk; website : www.amadeuspress.co.uk

ISBN : 978-1-902953-29-8

Front cover : Princes Dock is the setting for this view of the ***Leinster*** (4115grt/48) in summer 1968. She was ordered from the Harland & Wolff shipyard in Belfast in December 1945. She was launched on 20 May 1947 and delivered on 25 March 1948. She and sistership ***Munster*** took up service on the British & Irish Coast Lines route between Liverpool and Dublin on 5 April 1948. In addition to refrigerated space, both ships had stalls for 480 cattle. These were loaded in Dublin and discharged at the lairage at Birkenhead Woodside before the ships crossed the Mersey to Princes Dock. B&I was sold by Coast Lines to the Irish government in January 1965. The ***Munster*** and the ***Leinster*** were displaced in 1967 by more modern roll-on/roll-off tonnage. After a period laid up in Birkenhead and briefly renamed ***Leinster I*** to release her name for a new vessel, the ***Leinster*** was sold to Greek operators Mediterranean Sun Lines and converted to a ferry able to carry 100 cars and 550 passengers. Named ***Aphrodite***, she was laid up at Perama in 1983 and eventually scrapped in 1987.

Back cover : The Elder Dempster Line passenger/cargo liner ***Aureol*** (14083grt/51) is seen at Liverpool's Pier Head in Autumn 1968. She was built by A Stephen & Sons Ltd, Glasgow, and was launched on 28 March 1951. She was handed over to Elder Dempster on 12 October 1951. She and her earlier sisters ***Apapa*** and ***Accra*** maintained a two-week service from Liverpool. However, when passenger services became increasingly unprofitable in the late 1960s her two sisters were sold and she was converted to a one-class liner with 451 berths in 1968. She made the last West Africa passenger sailing from Liverpool on 16 March 1972 and was transferred to operate from Southampton. She was laid up at Southampton in 1974 and was sold the following year and renamed ***Marianna VI*** to become an accommodation hostel at Jeddah and Rabegh. In 1990 she was laid up off Piraeus. On 5 June 2001 she arrived at Alang to be broken up.

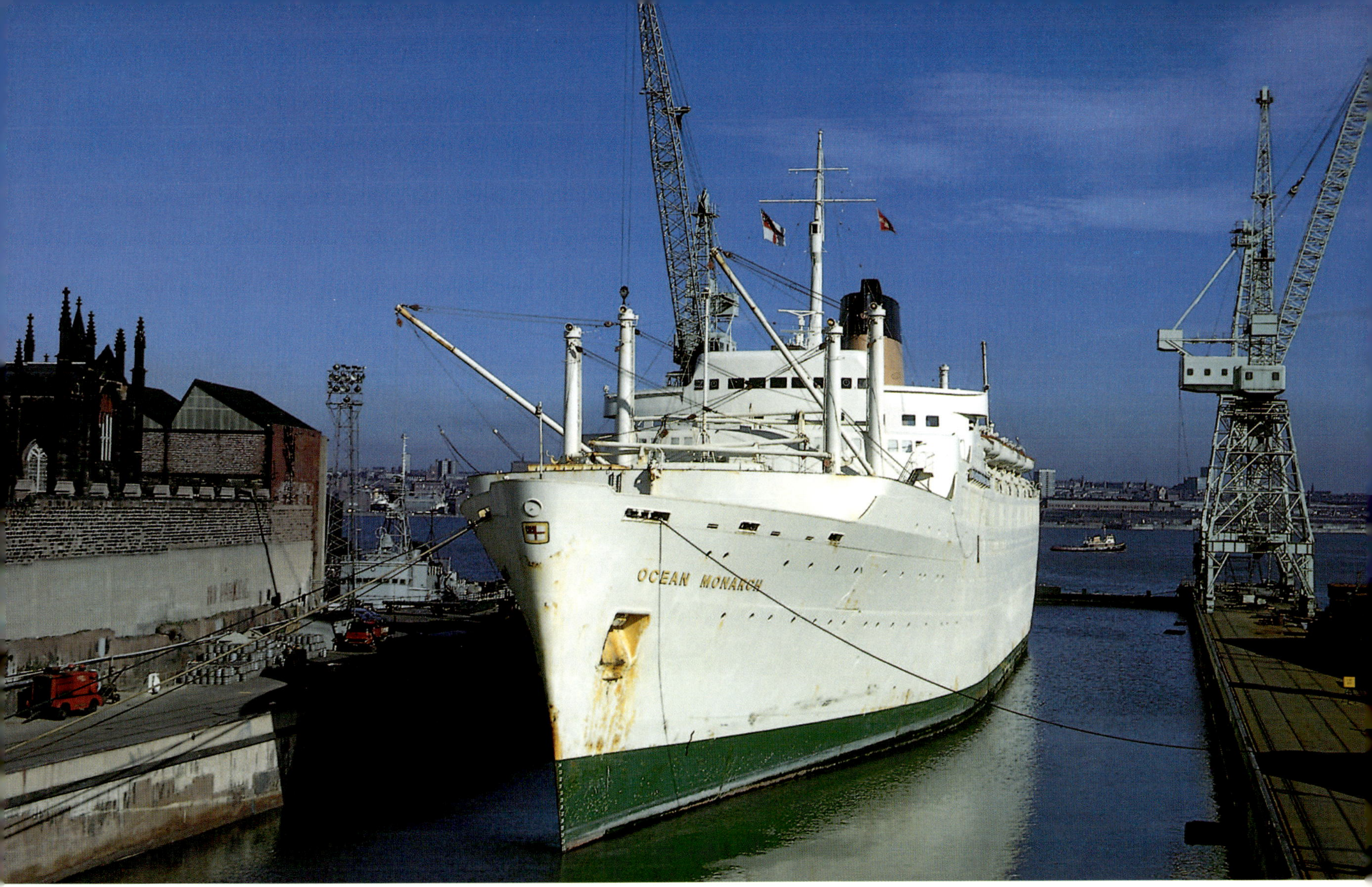

The ***Ocean Monarch*** (25971grt/57) is shown here in Cammell Laird's drydock in 1971 being refitted as a one-class cruise liner for Shaw Savill & Albion Co Ltd. She was originally built in 1957 as ***Empress of England*** for the Canadian Pacific Line and was chartered by the Travel Savings Association in 1963/64 to operate a series of cruises. She left Cammell Laird's yard for Southampton on 17 September 1971 and sailed on a Mediterranean cruise prior to operating on the United Kingdom to Australia and New Zealand service. In 1973 she was cruising out of Sydney but suffered persistent breakdowns and returned to the United Kingdom. She was withdrawn from service in 1975 and was broken up at Kaohsiung where she arrived on 17 July of that year.

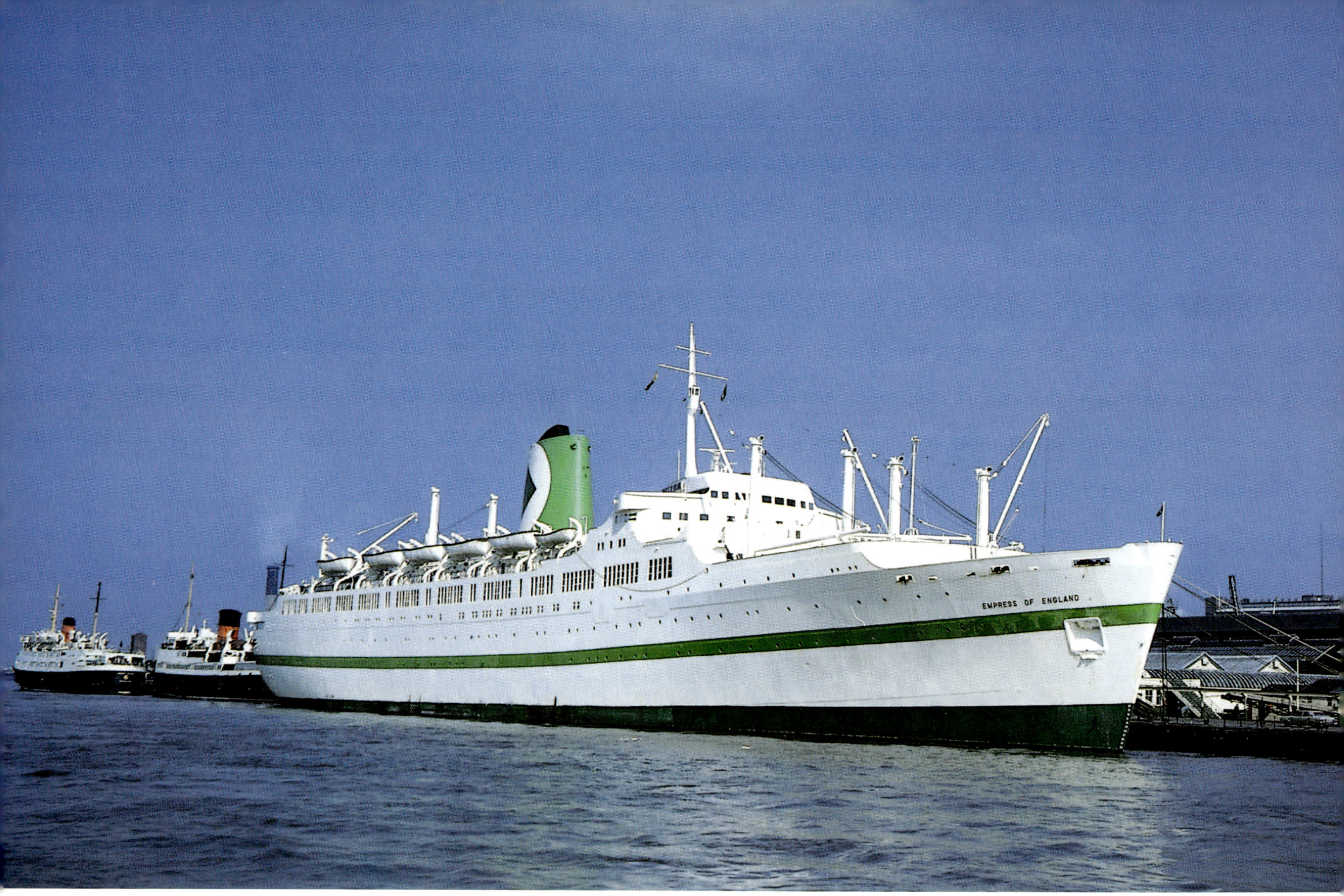

The ***Empress of England*** (25585grt/57) is seen here at the Liverpool Pier Head landing stage in Spring 1970. She is wearing the dreadful colour scheme inflicted on her in 1968; this should be compared to the splendid livery of the ***Empress of Canada*** on the next page. She was built at the Vickers-Armstrong shipyard at Walker on the River Tyne and launched on 9 May 1956, completion being in March 1957. The refit mentioned on page 3 proved to be a protracted affair, thanks largely to a series of strikes. She was to have a short career compared to the ***Empress of Canada*** and her sistership ***Empress of Britain*** which were the last of the famous Canadian Pacific "White Empresses" that were so well-known on the transatlantic routes.

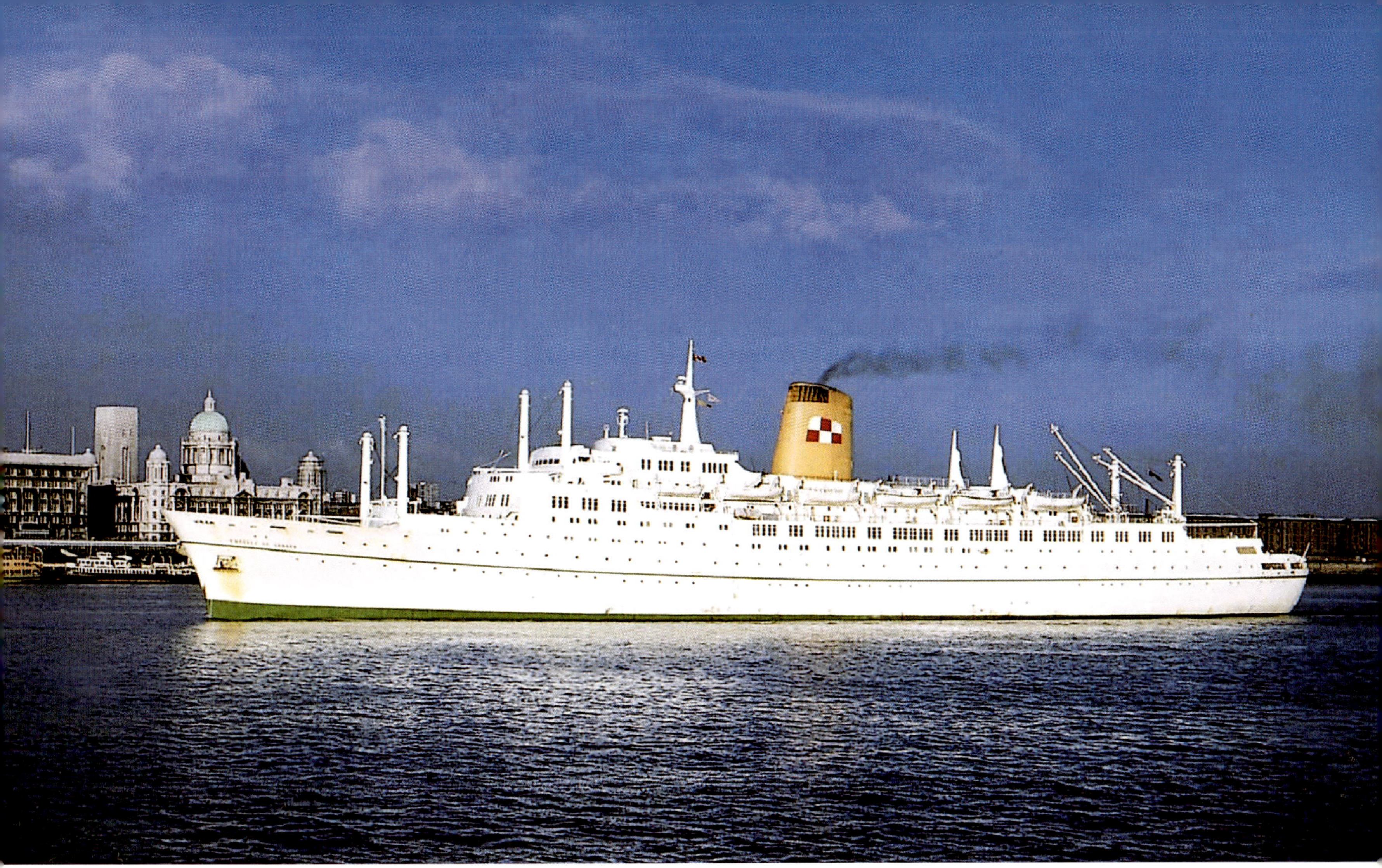

The Canadian Pacific liner ***Empress of Canada*** (25624grt/61) sails down the river to dock in Gladstone Dock in Spring 1970 after unloading passengers at Princes Landing Stage. A product of the Vickers-Armstrong shipyard on Tyneside, she was launched on 10 May 1960 and completed in April 1961. She left the Mersey on 24 April on her maiden voyage to Quebec and Montreal. She was built for the Liverpool to Montreal via Greenock service and she survived on that service until she was sold to Carnival Cruise Lines in 1972 and renamed ***Mardi Gras***. In 1993 she became the ***Olympic*** and was renamed ***Star of Texas*** in 1994. A charter by Direct Cruises brought her back to the Mersey in 1996 to operate a series of cruises to the Mediterranean as ***Apollon***. She was laid up at Eleusis in 2002 and was sold in late 2003 for demolition at Alang where she arrived on 9 December. It was reported that she was renamed ***Apollo*** during 2003 but she did not trade as such and the name was applied only for her final voyage to the breakers.

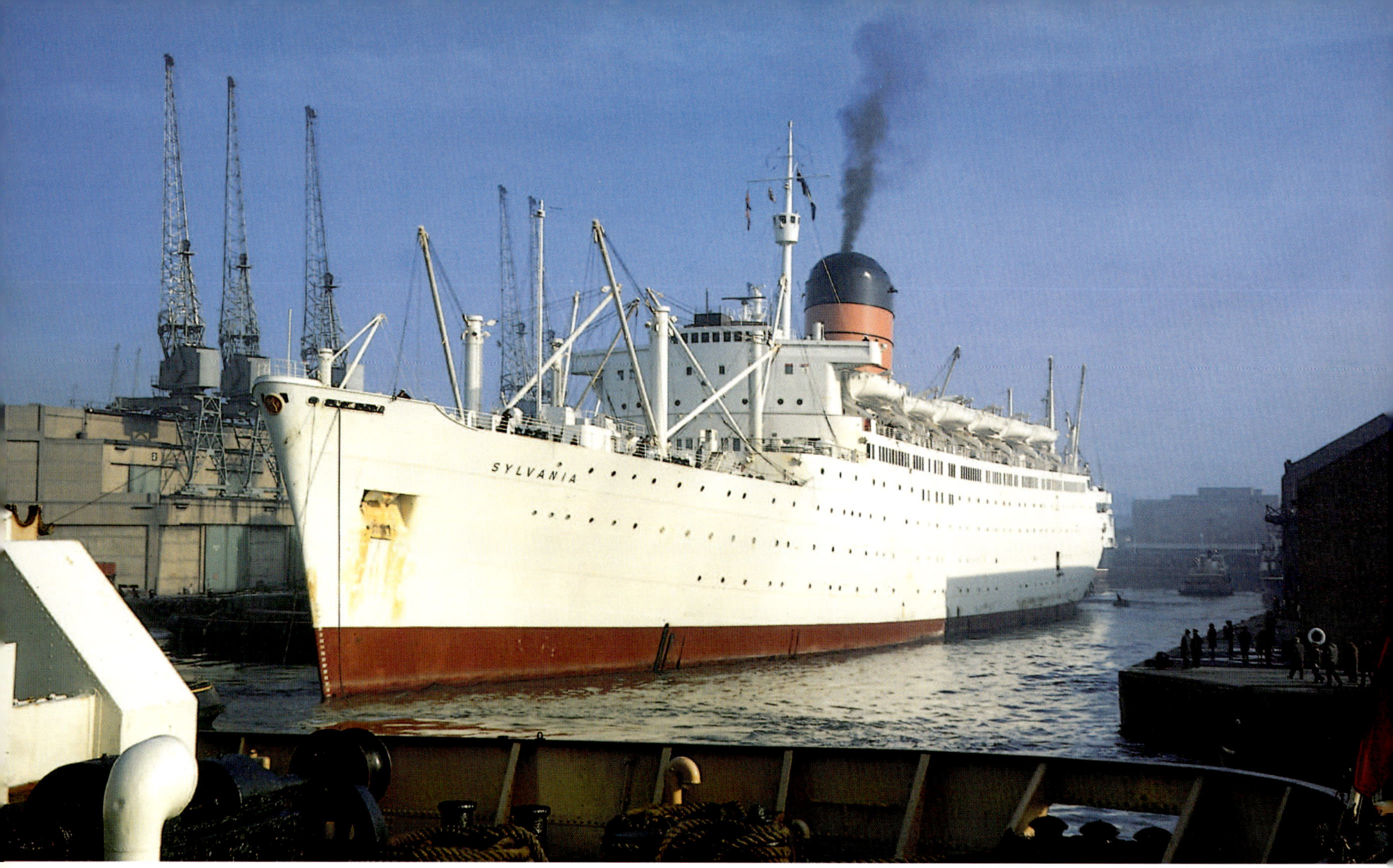

The ***Sylvania*** (22017grt/57) was the last of the four sisters built for the Cunard Line's Canadian service and sailed on her maiden voyage on 5 June 1957. She was built at the John Brown shipyard at Clydebank. Launched on 22 November 1956, she was handed over to Cunard in June 1957. In 1961 she replaced the ***Britannic*** on the Liverpool - New York route and in 1965 she made the first Cunard cruise out of Liverpool since 1939. The following year she took the final Cunard sailing out of Liverpool to New York and was painted with a white hull in 1967 as we see her in this photograph. The ***Sylvania*** was laid up in Southampton in 1967 and was sold with her sister ***Carinthia*** to Sitmar early the following year. She was renamed ***Fairwind*** and was rebuilt at Trieste in 1970. In 1988 she was briefly renamed ***Sitmar Fairwind*** before ***Dawn Princess***, becoming ***Albatros*** in 1993 and ***Genoa*** for the delivery voyage to the shipbreakers. She was beached at Alang on 10 January 2004 and subsequently was broken up.

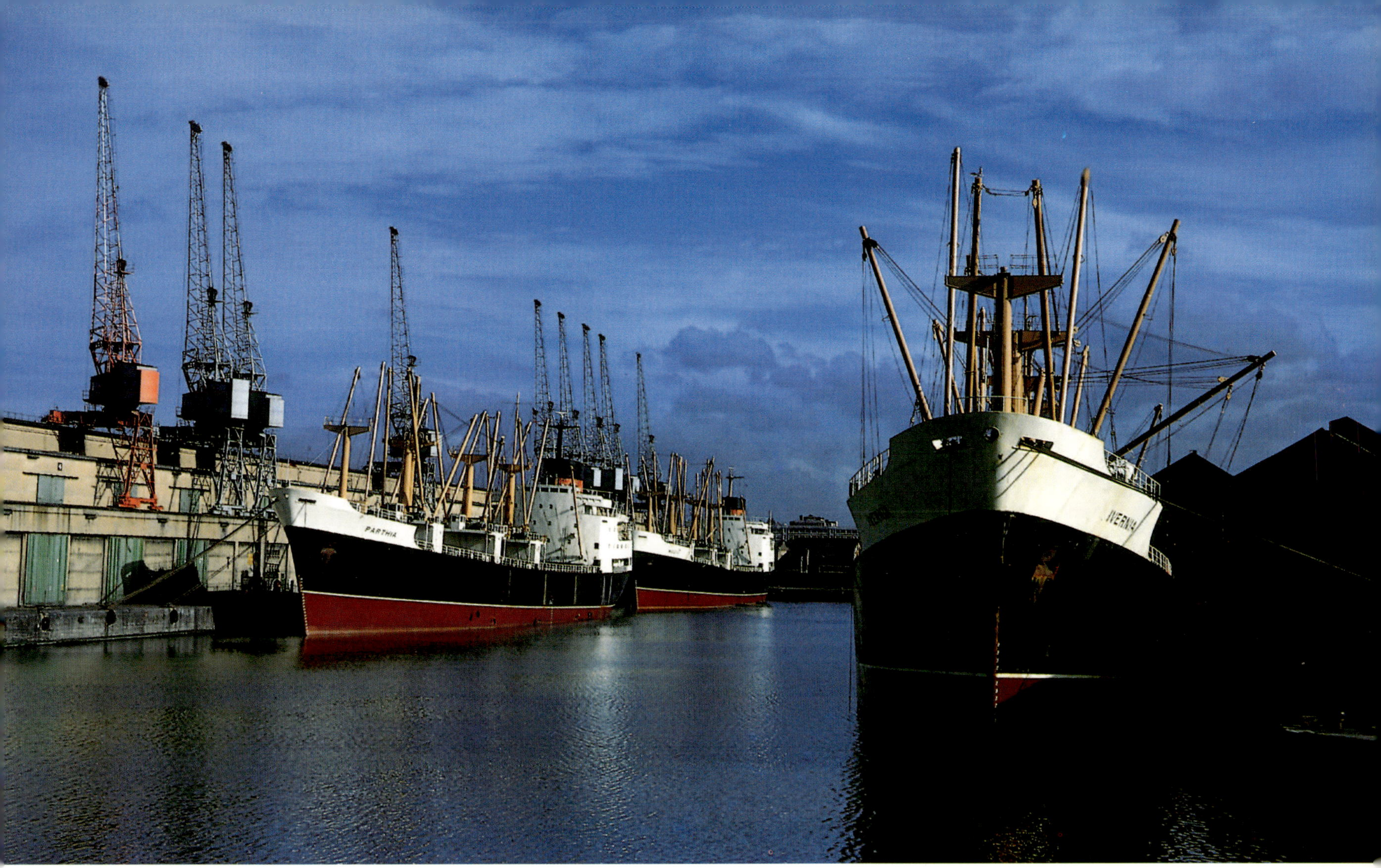

In addition to its well-known passenger vessels, the Cunard Line also had general cargo ships, three of which are seen here at the Line's berths in Huskisson Dock in Autumn 1970. The sisterships ***Parthia*** (5586grt/63) and ***Ivernia*** (5586grt/64) certainly started life together, both built by Robb Caledon at Dundee, but they had very different careers. The ***Parthia***, launched on 18 July 1963, had a relatively short life with Cunard, being sold in 1971 to the Western Australia Coastal Shipping Commission by whom she was renamed ***Wambiri*** and then ***Staship 1***. Sold again in 1979, she was renamed ***Rice Trader***. On 27 January 1984, she suffered engine failure off Socotra and was towed to Djibouti. Deemed unworthy of repair, she was towed to India later in that year and was broken up at Gadani Beach. By contrast, the ***Ivernia***, launched on 28 January 1964, was lengthened by 24 metres and transferred to the joint Cunard - Brocklebank Line in 1970 and was renamed ***Manipur***. We see her as such on page 28.

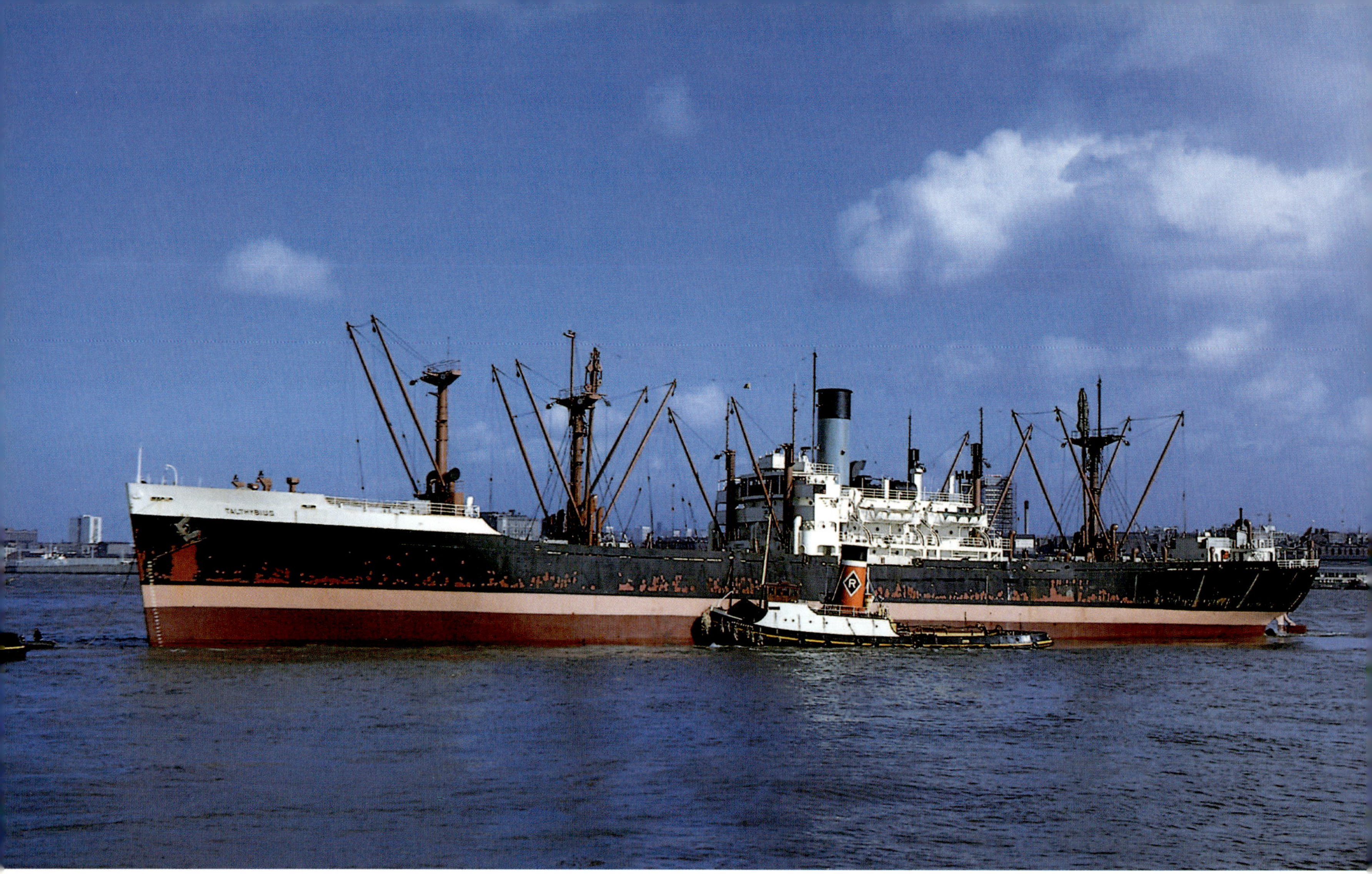

Photographed in late Summer 1968, Blue Funnel's ***Talthybius*** (7713grt/44) was built by Permanente Metals (Shipyard No. 1) at Richmond, California, as ***Salina Victory*** for the United States War Shipping Administration. She was launched on 24 November 1944, and was completed and handed over just one month later. She was one of six Victory ships purchased by the Blue Funnel group in 1946 to replace war losses. She went into the ownership of the Dutch associate of Blue Funnel, Nederlandse Stoomvaart Maatschappij Oceaan and took the name ***Polydorus*** and was not renamed ***Talthybius*** until 1960 when she was transferred to the Ocean Steam Ship Company of Liverpool. She was demolished in Kaohsiung following arrival there on 4 December 1971. She had seen ownership transferred briefly to Elder Dempster Lines Ltd and then Glen Line Ltd earlier in 1971. She is seen in the Mersey with the tug ***Applegarth*** in close company.

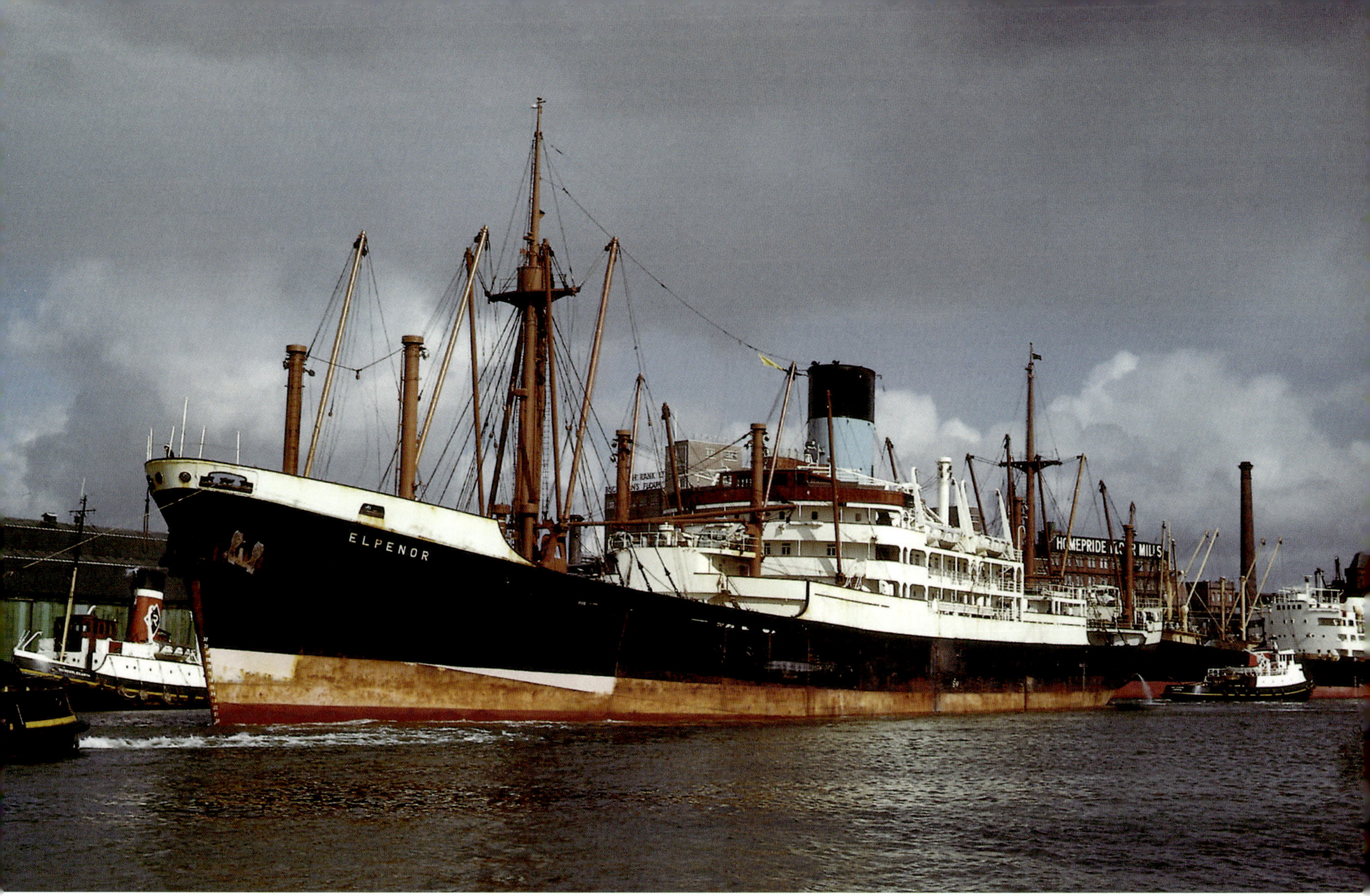

The ***Elpenor*** (7754grt/54) is towed through the Birkenhead dock system by Rea tugs. Built by Harland & Wolff at Belfast, she was launched on 11 November 1953 and completed on 22 April 1954. She was powered by a 7-cylinder B&W engine manufactured by her builder. Like many vessels of her generation, she was able to carry a small quantity of liquid cargo, having deep tanks for the carriage of vegetable oil and a poop tank able to carry a similar cargo or latex. She operated for the Blue Funnel Line until being briefly transferred to Elder Dempster Line prior to her sale to Cremorne Bay Shipping Company, Liberia, in 1977. Renamed ***United Concord***, she operated for them for a year and was broken up at Kaohsiung where she arrived on 21 May 1979.

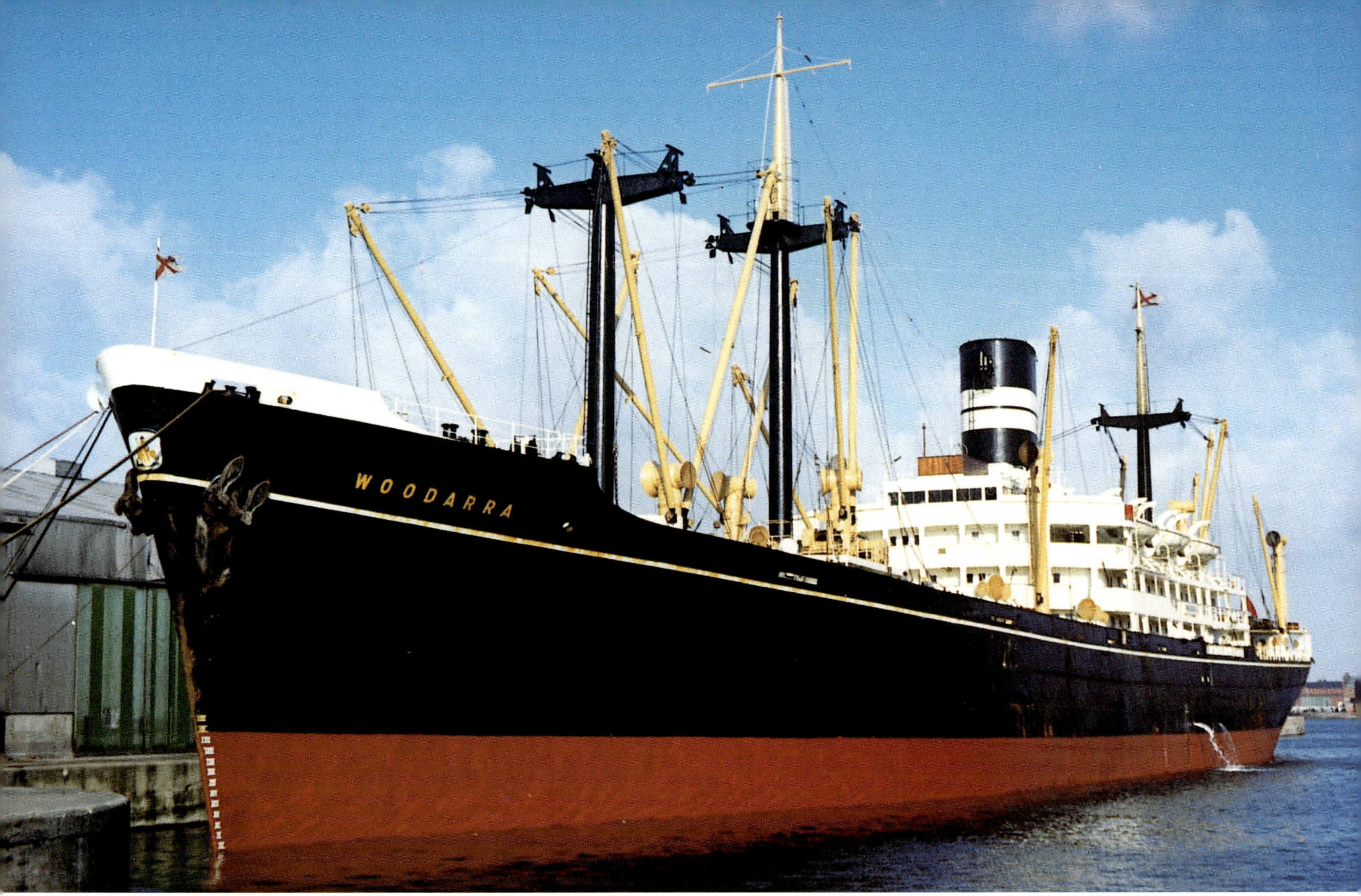

Ships of the British India Steam Navigation Co Ltd were rare visitors to the Mersey. The ***Woodarra*** (8753grt/57) is shown berthed in Brocklebank Dock following an overhaul. She was launched into the River Clyde on 22 November 1956 at the Whiteinch shipyard of Barclay, Curle & Co Ltd on the River Clyde and was completed in April 1957. She operated as ***Woodarra*** until 1968 when she became ***Pando Gulf*** for the P&O Far East service. In 1974 she was sold to the Ben Line and renamed ***Benalbanach*** and was broken up at Inchon in May 1978.

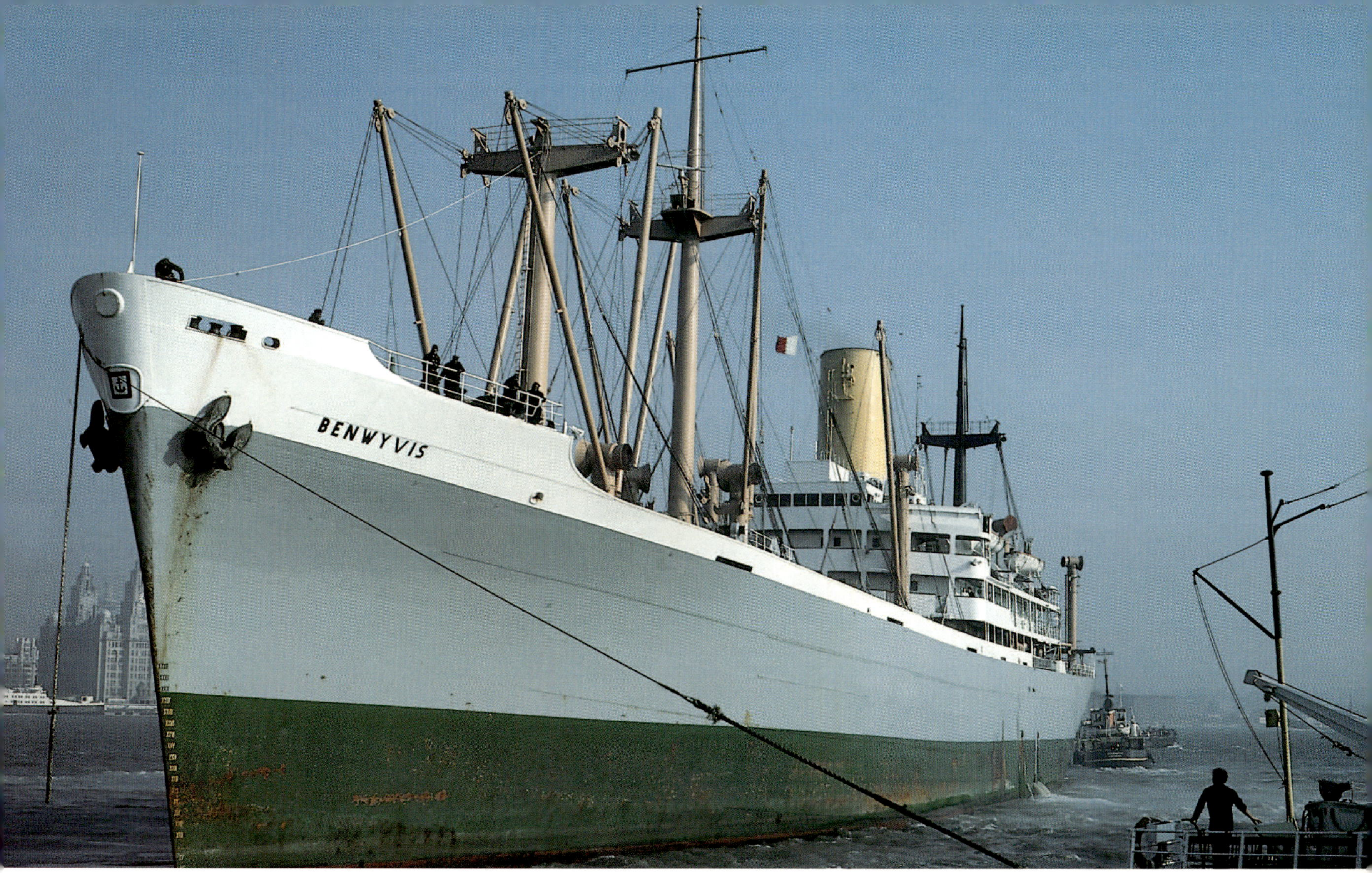

The ***Benwyvis*** (8753grt/57), a sistership of the ***Woodarra***, approaches the Alfred Dock river entrance in October 1977. She was the fifth vessel to carry this name in the Ben Line fleet. Similarly built at the Barclay, Curle yard, she was launched on 28 May 1957 and handed over to owners British India Steam Navigation Co Ltd on 6 September of that same year. She was named ***Waroonga*** but became ***Pando Point*** in 1969, British India having been taken over by Peninsula & Oriental (P&O) the previous year. She joined the Ben Line fleet in July 1974. This photograph shows her at the end of her career for she was arriving to lay up prior to sale for demolition. Her final voyage took her to Kaohsiung where she arrived for scrapping on 30 January 1978.

(C J Tabarin)

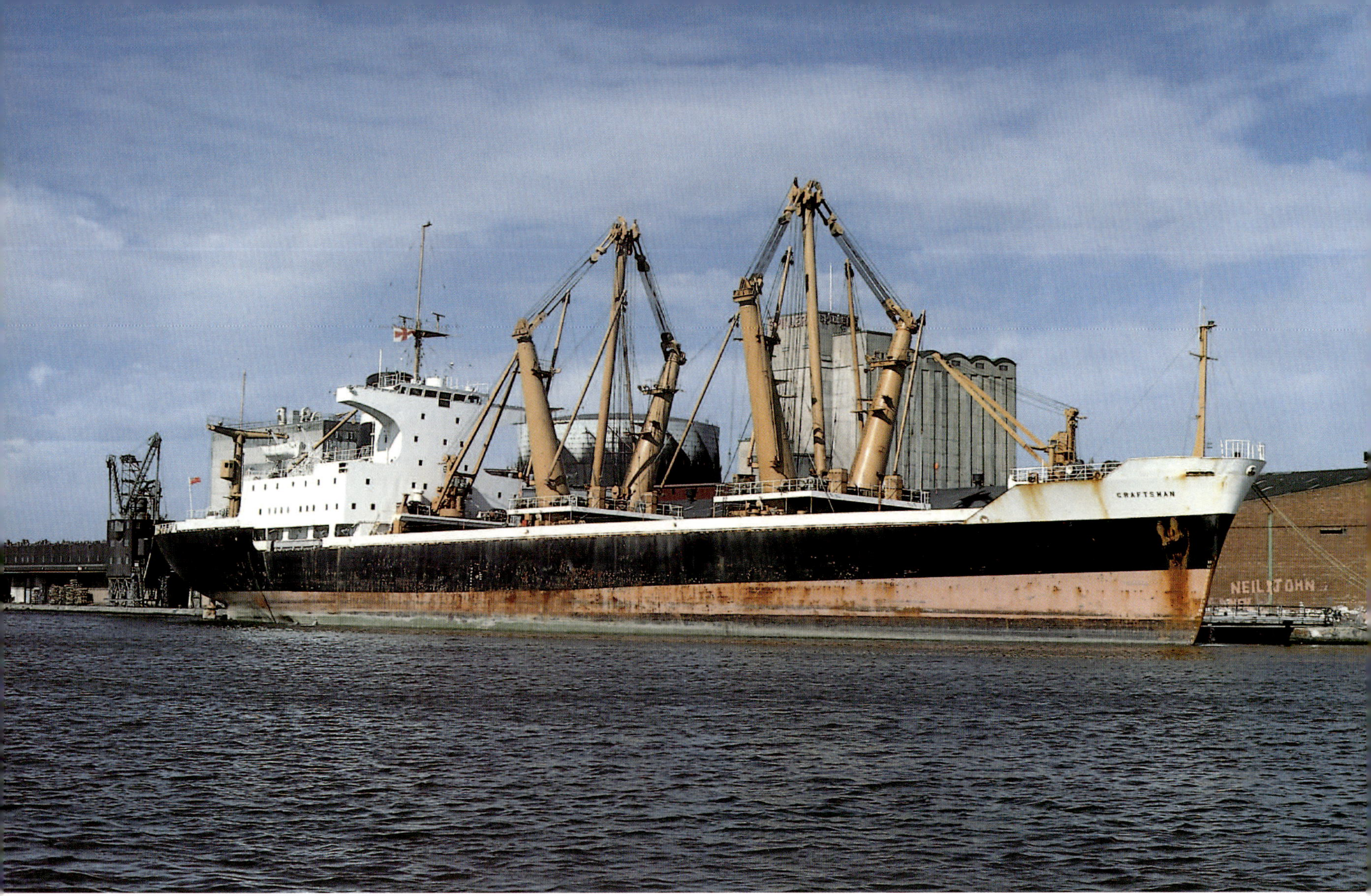

The ***Craftsman*** (10220grt/72) is loading cargo in the West Float at Birkenhead. She was built at the Wm Doxford yard in Sunderland and was launched on 23 June 1971. A strike at the building yard meant that she was not delivered until 28 February 1972. In addition to other cargo handling gear, she was equipped with two 250-ton Stülcken derricks. She is seen here in Spring 1981. Later in the year she was sold by Harrison Line to Ierax Shipping of Greece and renamed ***Forum Craftsman***, owned by the Forum Maritime Group. She later became ***Royal Crusader*** in 1988 and ***Christina J*** in 1992, eventually being broken up at Cebu in the Philippines, where she arrived on 18 August 1994.

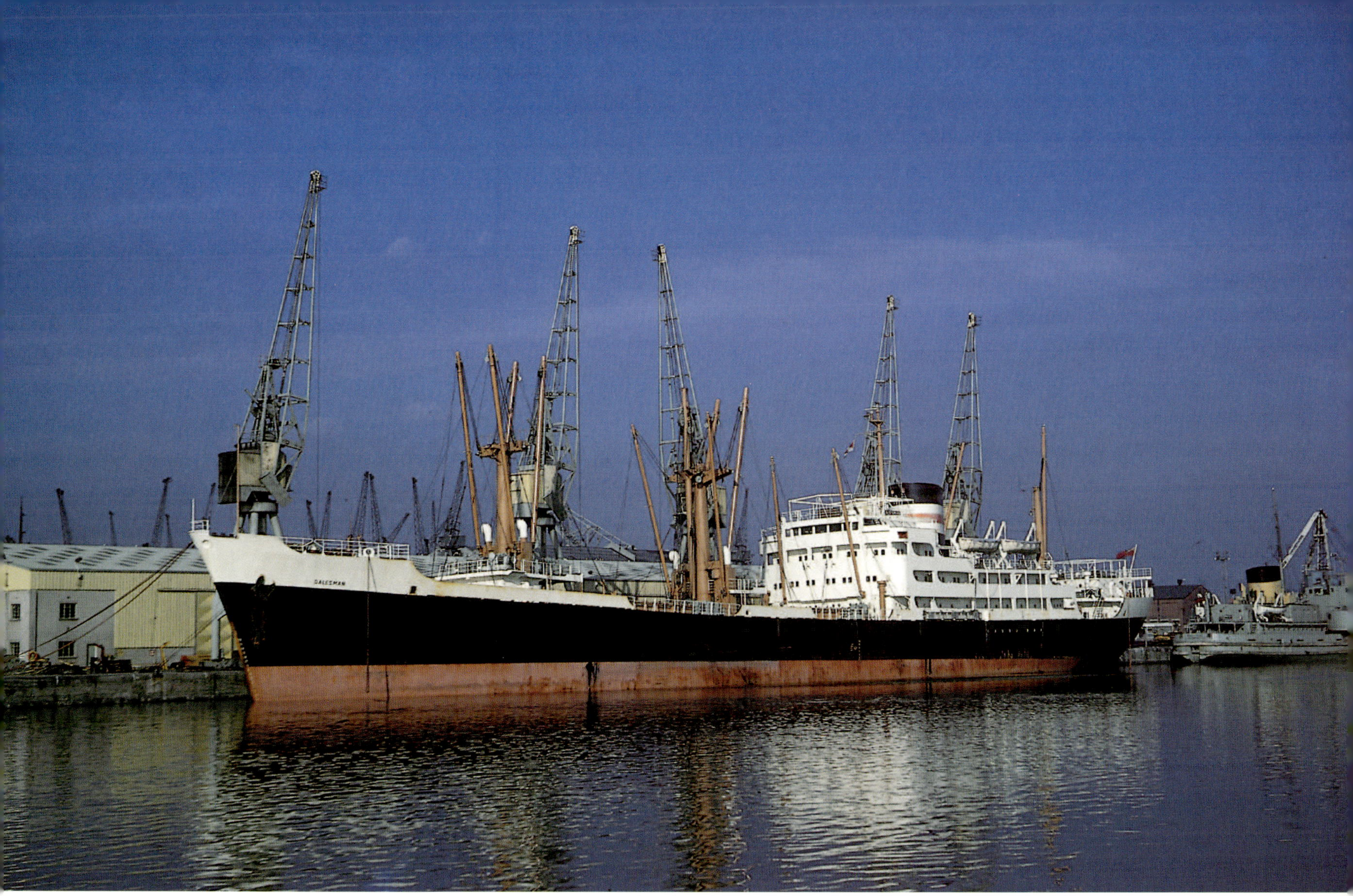

The ***Dalesman*** (7200grt/61), loading cargo at Liverpool in 1972, exemplifies an earlier design of Harrison Line ship. She was built in 1961 by the Nederlandse Dok & Scheepsbouw in Amsterdam. Launched on 15 June 1961, she was handed over to Harrison Line on 2 November 1961 and remained in the fleet until sold to Tembo Shipping Company of Greece in 1979 and renamed ***Adrianos***. She became ***Ioannis*** in 1980 and was laid up at Piraeus on 4 October 1982. Early in 1984 she was reactivated for a delivery voyage to Chinese ship breakers at Huangpu where she arrived on 14 April.

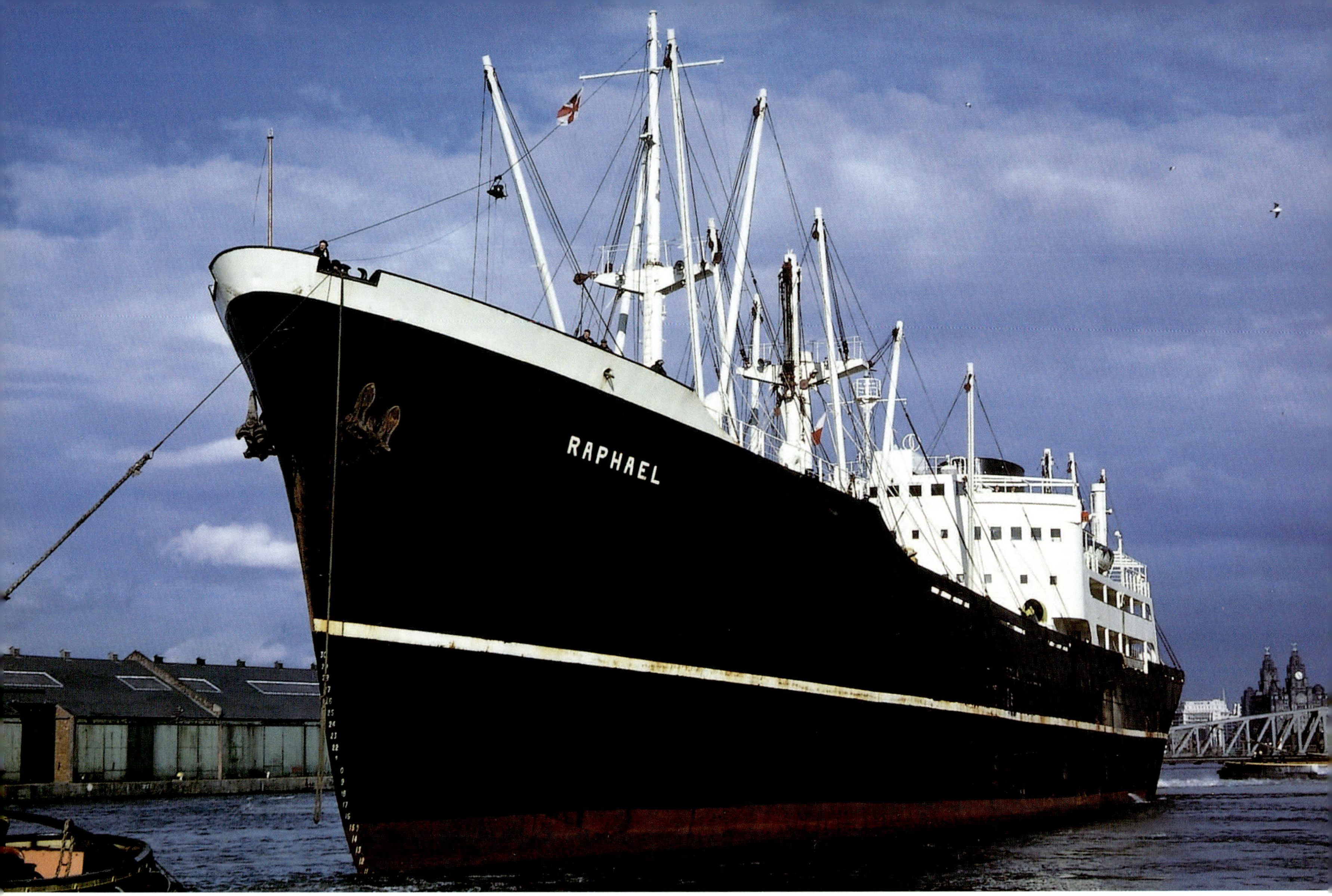

The Lamport & Holt cargo vessel ***Raphael*** (7971grt/53) is seen in Birkenhead Docks on charter to the Harrison Line during 1968. Built by Bartram & Sons Ltd at Sunderland, she was launched on 16 March 1953. When she was delivered, she was the line's fastest ship with a service speed of 17.5 knots thanks to her Doxford 2-stroke 6-cylinder diesel engine. After a successful career trading to South America she was sold in 1976 becoming ***Pola Rika*** and in 1979 she was sold to shipbreakers at Gijon, arriving at this Spanish port in May 1979.

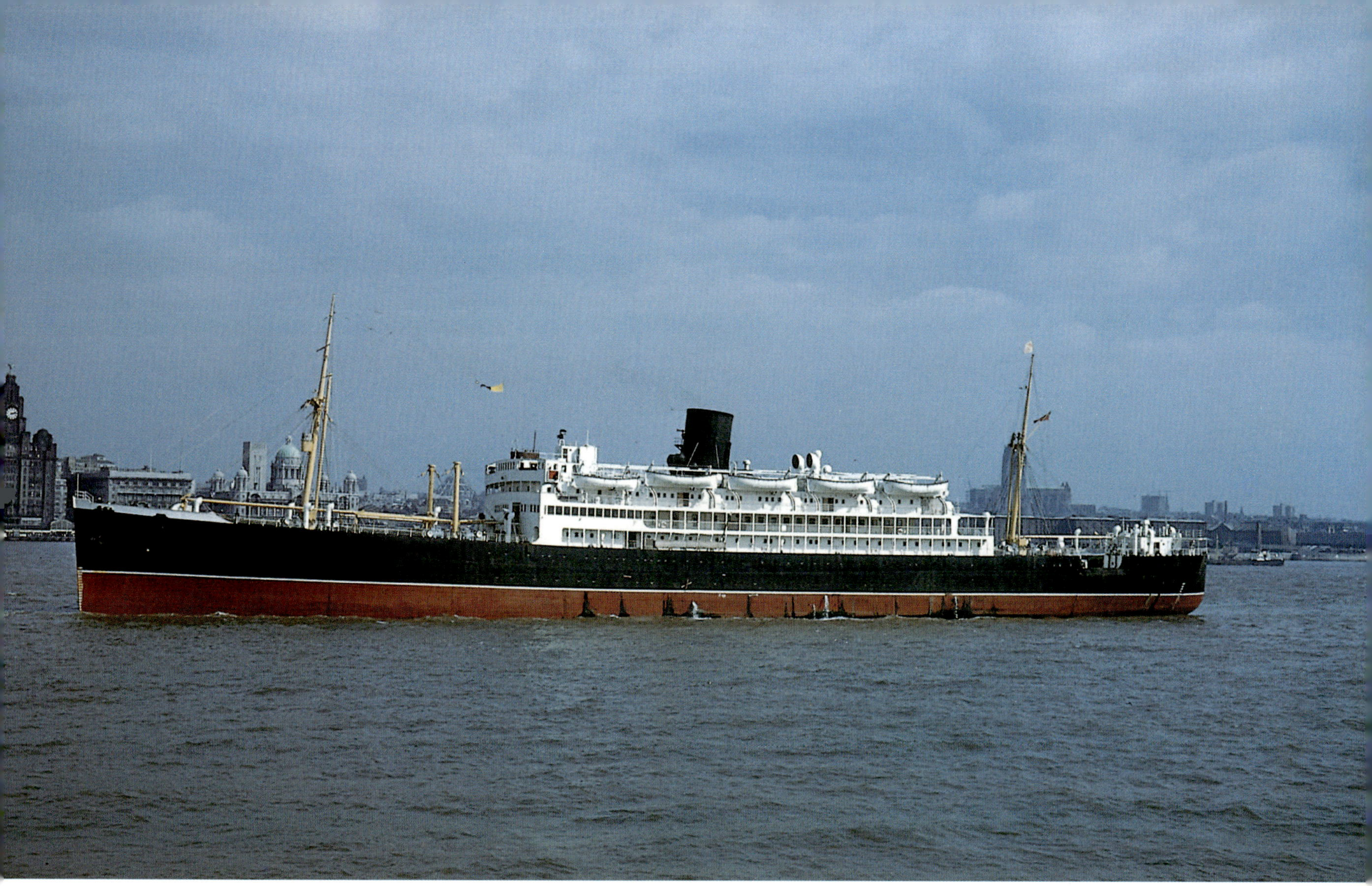

Anchor Line's ***Circassia*** (11170grt/37) is seen in the River Mersey off Alfred Dock in mid-1964. She was built at the Clydeside yard of Fairfield Co Ltd for the service from Glasgow and Liverpool to Bombay with accommodation for 300 first class and 80 steerage passengers. She was launched on 8 June 1937 and completed in October of that year. She is of special interest as being an early example of a Doxford-engined motor vessel, having two 2-stroke 4-cylinder engines. ***Circassia*** was converted to an Armed Merchant Cruiser in 1940 and became a troopship in 1942. The following year she was rebuilt as a Landing Ship Infantry and was returned to the Anchor Line in 1947. She made the last Anchor Line passenger sailing to Bombay from Glasgow and Liverpool in January 1966 and arrived at Alicante on 25 April to be broken up.

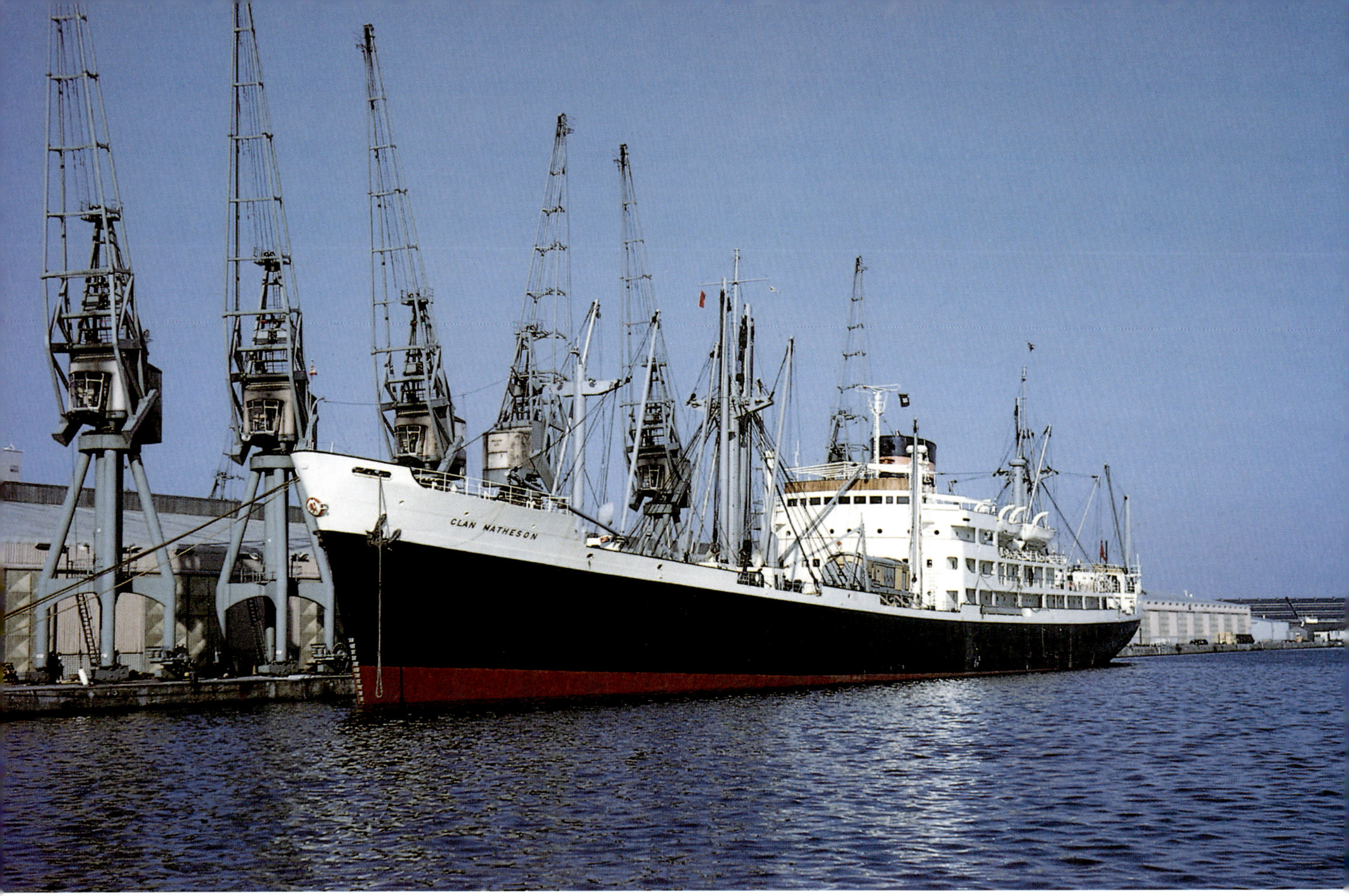

The ***Clan Matheson*** (7553grt/57) is loading cargo at Berth 215 in Vittoria Dock, Birkenhead in Summer 1972, prior to sailing to Aden, Bombay, Cochin, Tuticorin, Madras and Chittagong in 1970. She carries a diesel locomotive as deck cargo. She is a further example of a cargo liner powered by a Doxford engine, a 2-stroke 6-cylinder example. Like so many Clan Line ships, she was built by the Greenock Dockyard Co Ltd. She was launched on 26 August 1957 and completed four months later. In the mid-1970s, she served as Clan Line's cadet ship. After a comparatively short life of only twenty one years, she arrived at Kaohsiung on 12 December 1978 to be broken up.

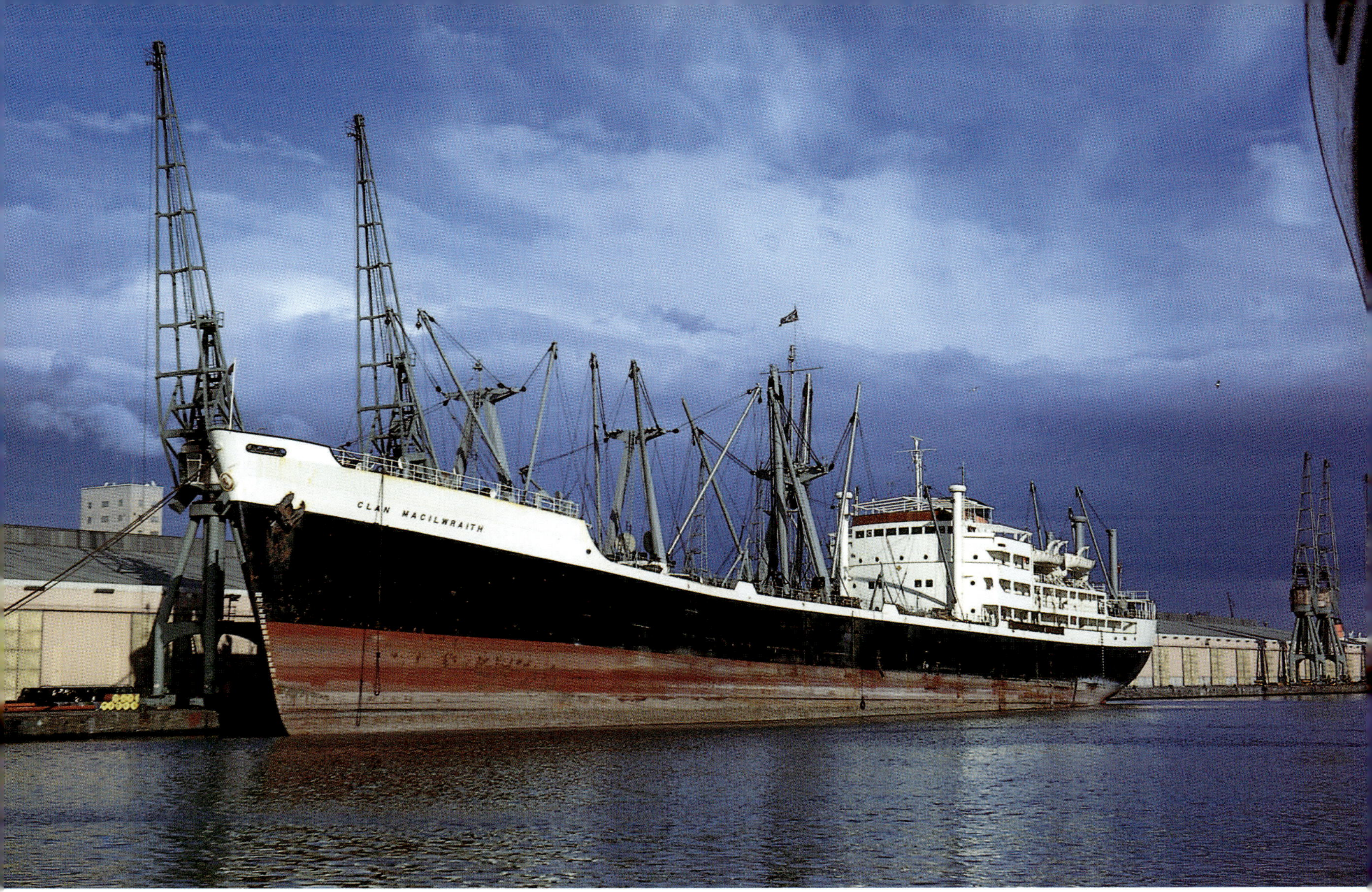

Clan Line's ***Clan Macilwraith*** (7419grt/60) is also berthed at Berth 215 in Vittoria Dock at Birkenhead prior to entering drydock for annual overhaul in Spring 1973. The three members of her class were built with distinctive bipod masts again by the Greenock Dockyard Company on the Clyde. Launched on 17 June 1960, she was handed over in December of that year. Her 2-stroke 5-cylinder Doxford engine gave her a speed of only 14 knots compared to the 16.5 knots of the ***Clan Matheson***. She was sold to Guan Guan Shipping Limited, Singapore, in 1979 and renamed ***Golden City***. On 17 July 1986 her No. 1 hold caught fire in the Malacca Strait and when she arrived at Singapore the remaining cargo was discharged. She was declared a total loss and scrapped at Jurong where she arrived in October 1986.

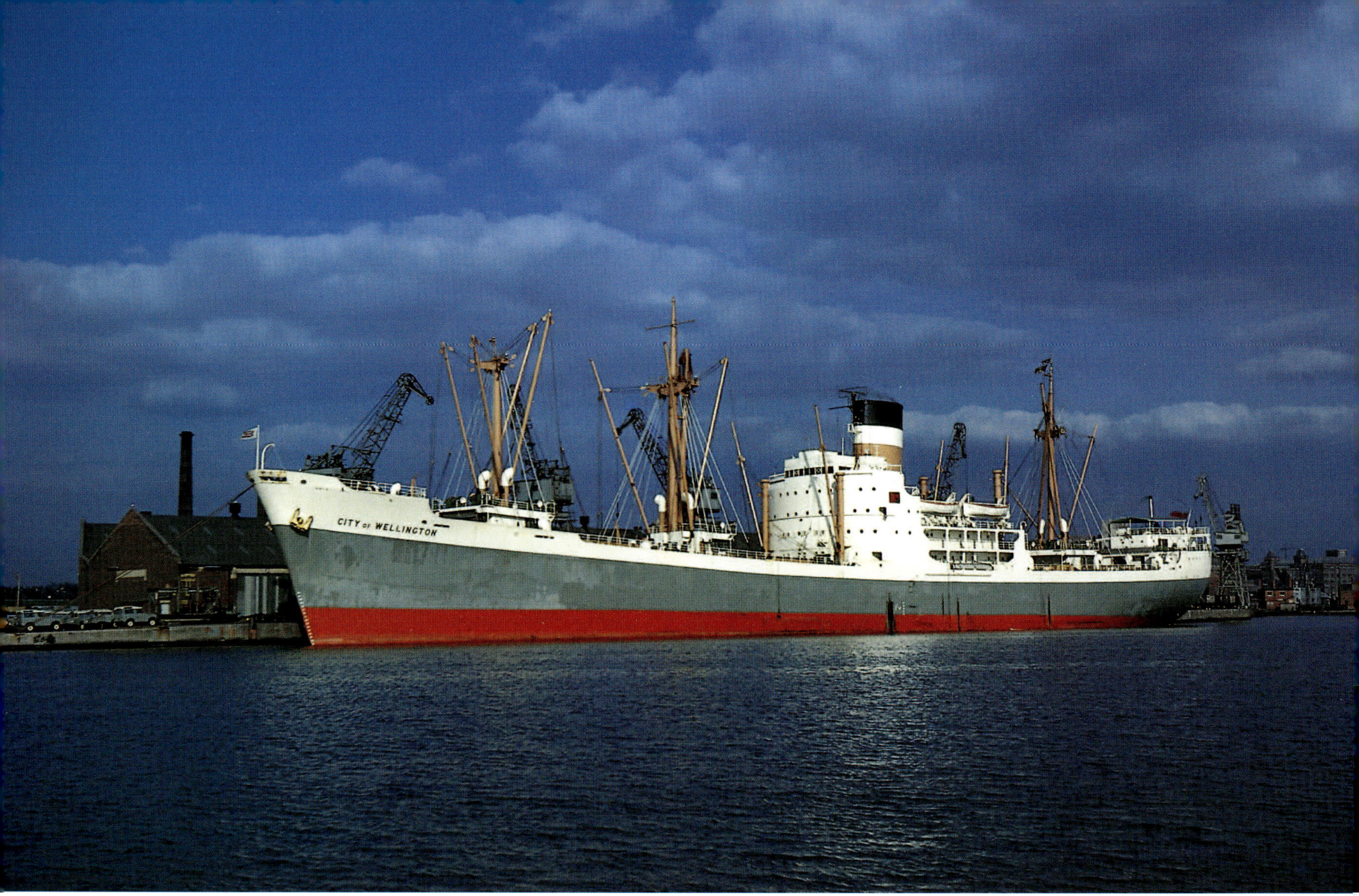

Ellerman Hall Line's vessel ***City of Wellington*** (7702grt/56) at the loading berth, Berth 223, in the West Float at Birkenhead in April 1973. A product of the Cammell Laird yard at Birkenhead, she was launched on 31 January 1956 but not completed until October of that year. She is yet another cargo liner from the mid-1950s to be powered by a Doxford 2-stroke 6-cylinder engine. In 1973 following a reorganisation in the Ellerman Group she was transferred to the Ellerman City Lines division and was sold to Mulroy Bay Shipping in 1978 and renamed ***Eastern Enterprise***. On 13 February the following year she arrived at Kaohsiung to be broken up.

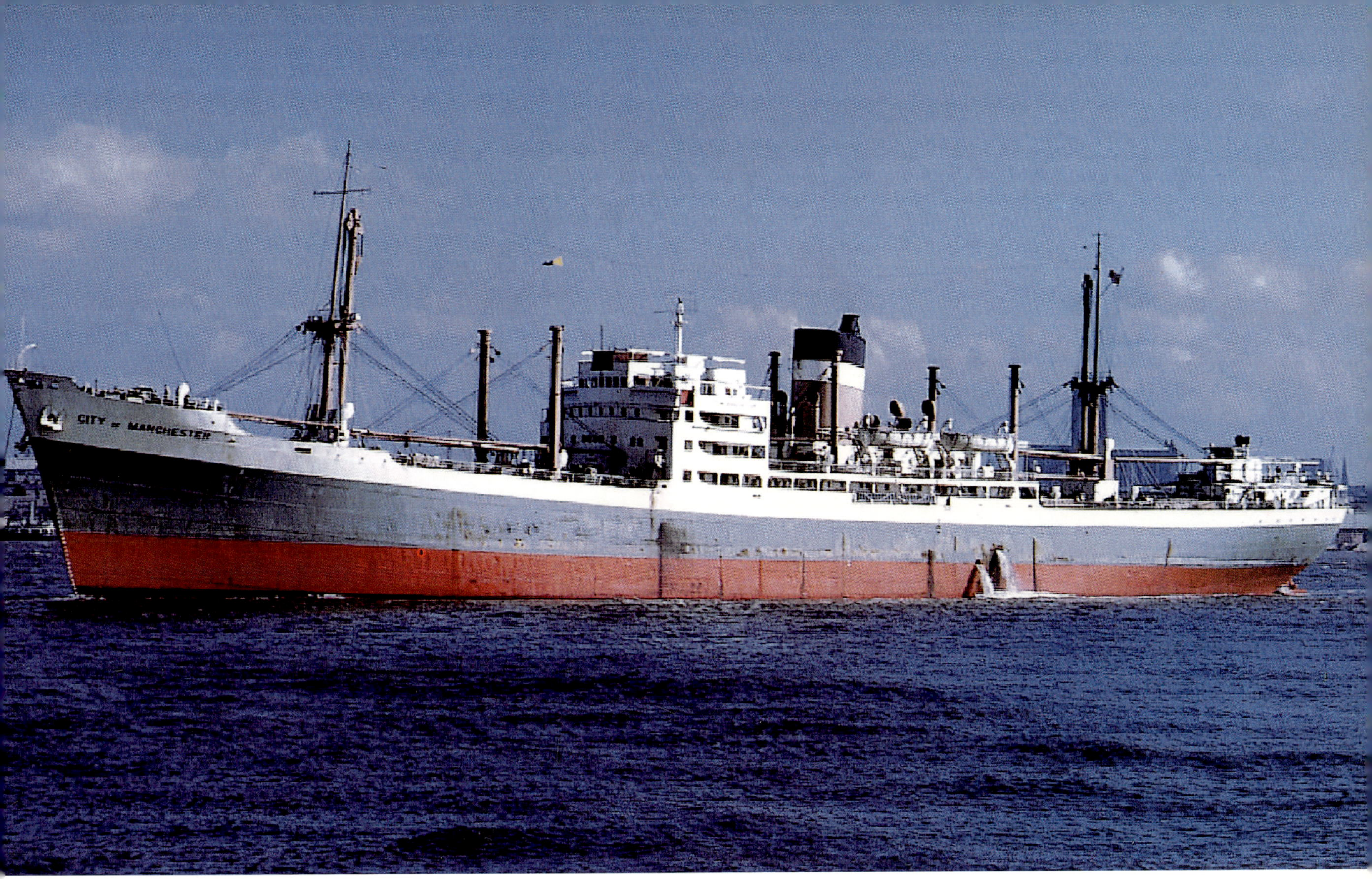

Ellerman City Line's ***City of Manchester*** (7585grt/50) enters the Birkenhead Dock system at Alfred Dock in 1969 to load cargo for Indian and Pakistani ports. She was built at the J L Thompson shipyard in Sunderland where she was launched on 9 August 1949, completion being in March of the following year. She had the misfortune to be involved in a tragic accident even before she entered service. Her three steam turbine engines were fitted on the Tyne and as she was being towed back to Sunderland on 11 February 1950, she was caught by heavy winds and was being driven westwards offshore. One of her tugs, the ***Stag*** (148grt/1897) was pulled over and sank in heavy seas with the loss of four of her six-strong crew. She went on to serve the Ellerman Group until 1971 when she was sold for £90,000 to Kavo Cia. Naviera S.A., Panama, and was renamed ***Kavo Yerakas***. She was broken up at Kaohsiung later that year, having arrived on 6 November.

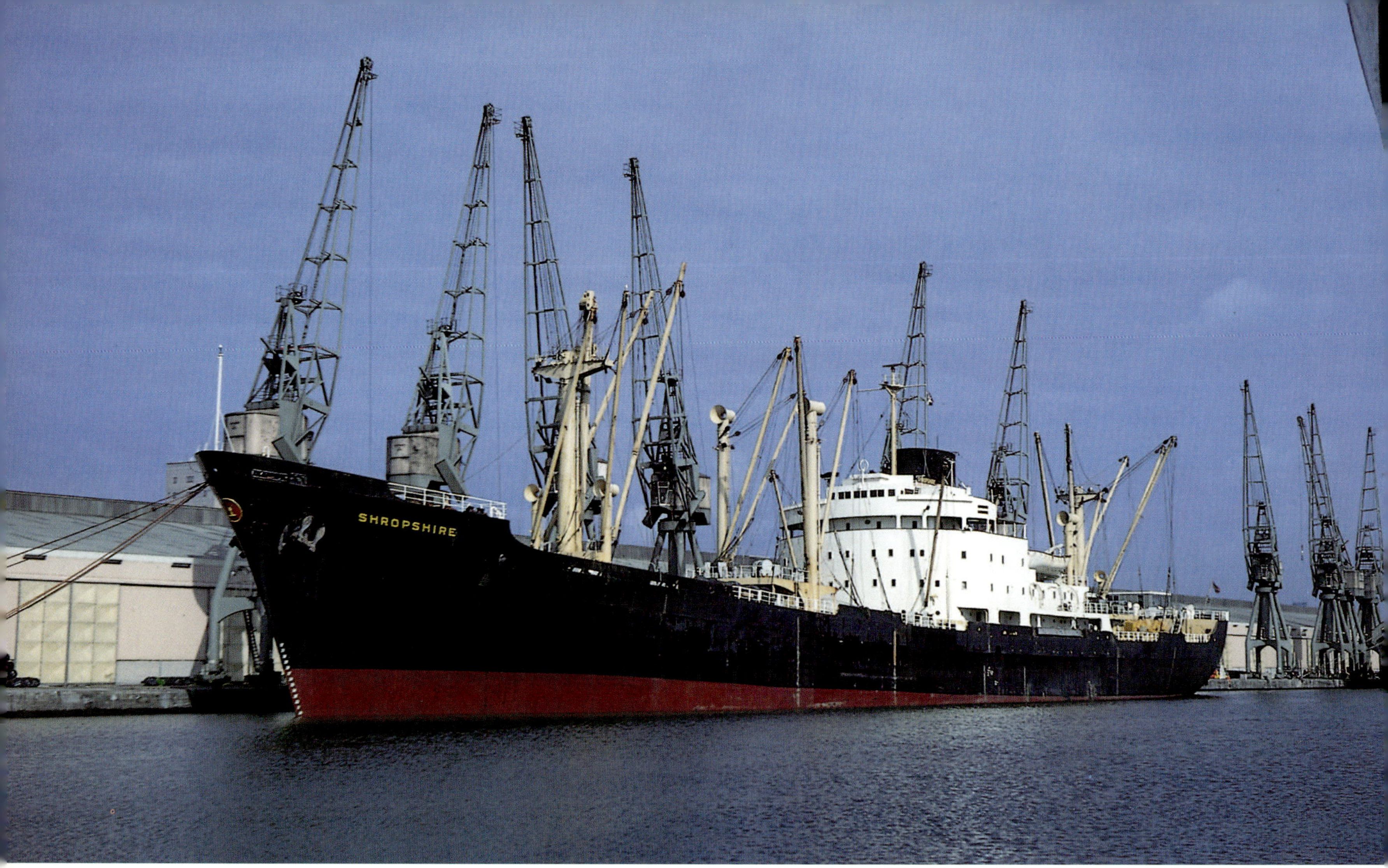

Bibby Line's cargo vessel ***Shropshire*** (7244grt/59) was built by the Fairfield Shipbuilding & Engineering Company at its yard in Govan on the River Clyde and was launched on 14 November 1958. She was completed in April of the following year. Here we see her in 1968 as she was loading at Berth 215 in Vittoria Dock, Birkenhead. The ***Shropshire*** and her sister ***Cheshire*** were delivered in 1959 for the Bibby Line service to Egypt, Sri Lanka and Burma (Myanmar) although they spent most of their lives chartered to other operators. ***Shropshire*** was sold to Lefkonia Cia. Naviera S.A., Panama, in 1972 and renamed ***Argiro***. In October 1981 she arrived at Piraeus and was laid up until 1984 when she was again sold and given the name ***Naftilos*** and loaded a cargo for India. She arrived at Chittagong on 6 March the following year and was broken up.

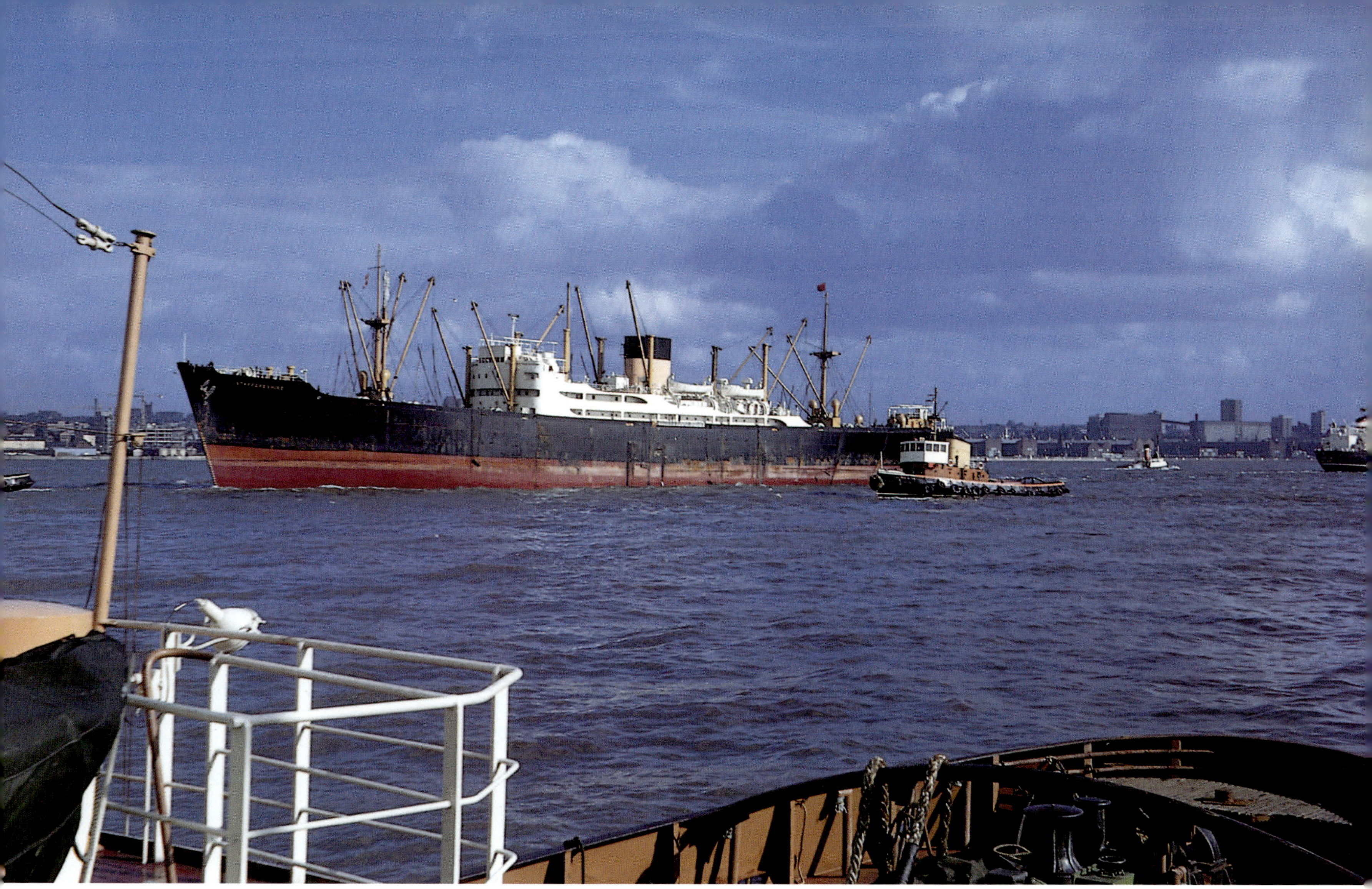

On an autumn day in 1968, Liverpool Screw Towing Company tugs assist the Bibby Line cargo vessel ***Staffordshire*** (8808grt/50) into Alfred Dock, Birkenhead, where she would load for India and Pakistan. The ***Staffordshire*** was built at the Tyneside yard of Vickers-Armstrong and launched on 31 May 1950. She was handed over to original owners Prince Line as ***Eastern Prince*** in October 1950. Renamed ***Bardic*** between 1960 and 1964, she was acquired by Bibby Line along with her sister ***Cingalese Prince*** in 1964 to replace the passenger/cargo liners ***Warwickshire*** and ***Leicestershire***. The ***Cingalese Prince*** was renamed ***Gloucestershire***. On 30 November 1970 during a voyage from Birkenhead to Rangoon (Yangon), the ***Staffordshire*** had to put into Colombo with engine problems and was broken up at Hong Kong the following year, arriving on 6 March 1971.

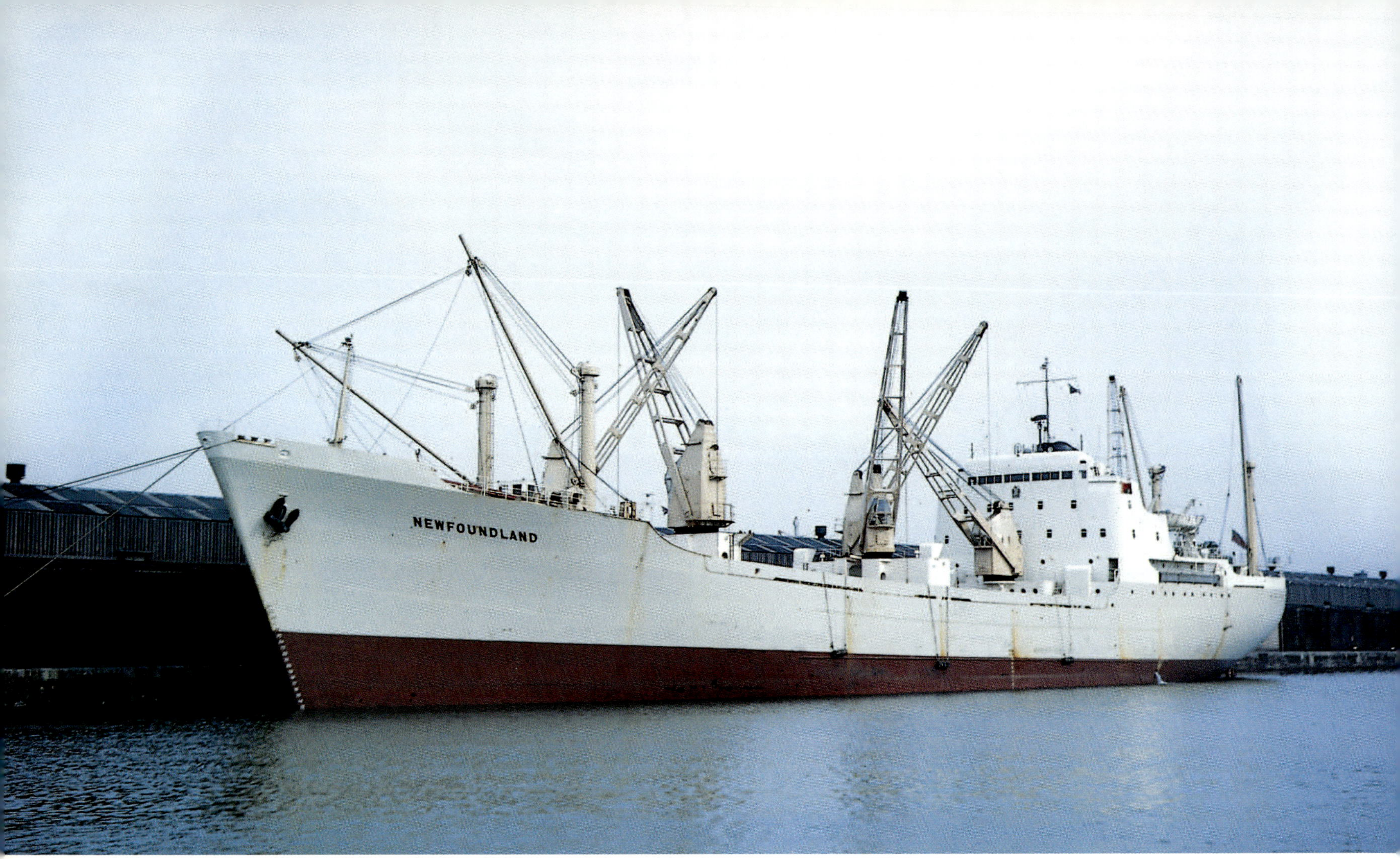

The ***Newfoundland*** (6660grt/64), photographed at Berth 80 in Alexandra Branch Dock No. 1, was one of a pair of sisterships built by the Burntisland Shipbuilding Co Ltd. She and her sistership ***Nova Scotia*** replaced two cargo/passenger ships of the same names which had worked on the Furness Withy service across the North Atlantic but the two new ships had no passenger accommodation. Both ships had names associated with the Johnston Warren Line, a constituent of the Furness Withy group, but they seem to have been owned by the parent company. In the mid-1970s, when shipping was undergoing huge changes as it began to cope with the impact of containerisation. They were transferred within the group and the ***Newfoundland*** was renamed ***Cufic*** in 1973, becoming ***Newfoundland*** again the following year, and then ***Cufic*** once more in 1975. ***Cufic***, incidentally, was a name associated with Shaw, Savill & Albion Co Ltd, another company within the Furness Withy group. The reality was, though, that such vessels were of no further use in the trades for which they had been built and she was sold for service in the Far East where she traded under the Panamanian flag as ***Gaiety***. She was eventually scrapped in Shanghai in 1986.

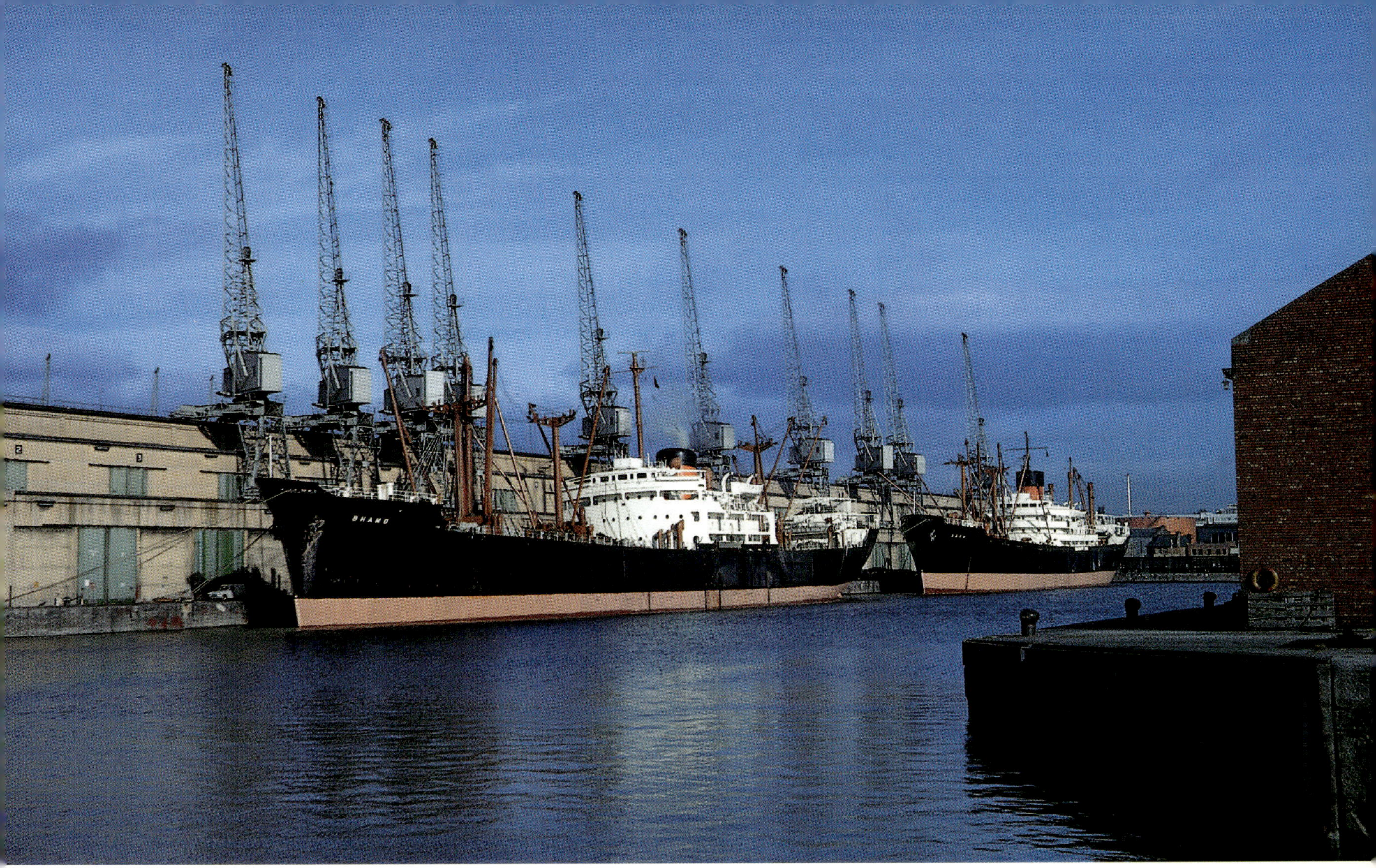

The ***Bhamo*** (5932grt/57) and ***Daru*** (6340grt/58) are loading cargo for West Africa in Liverpool's Huskisson Branch Dock No. 1 during 1971. The ***Bhamo*** was built at the Port Glasgow shipyard of Lithgows Ltd. Launched on 25 September 1957, she was handed over in December of that year to the British & Burmese Steam Navigation Company with Paddy Henderson as managers. She was transferred to the Henderson Line in 1964 and the Guinea Gulf Line in 1967. She was sold in 1979 becoming ***Bhamot*** for a final delivery voyage to Kaohsiung where she arrived on 6 July 1979. The ***Daru*** was built by Scotts' Shipbuilding & Engineering Co Ltd and was launched at this company's shipyard in Greenock on 10 April 1958. She was handed over to Elder Dempster Lines on 11 November 1958. She became ***Yoma*** in 1965 for a short time and reverted to ***Daru*** the same year. She was sold and renamed ***Lone Eagle*** in 1979 and then ***Anjo One*** in 1980. She was eventually broken up at Gadani Beach where she arrived on 14 February 1982.

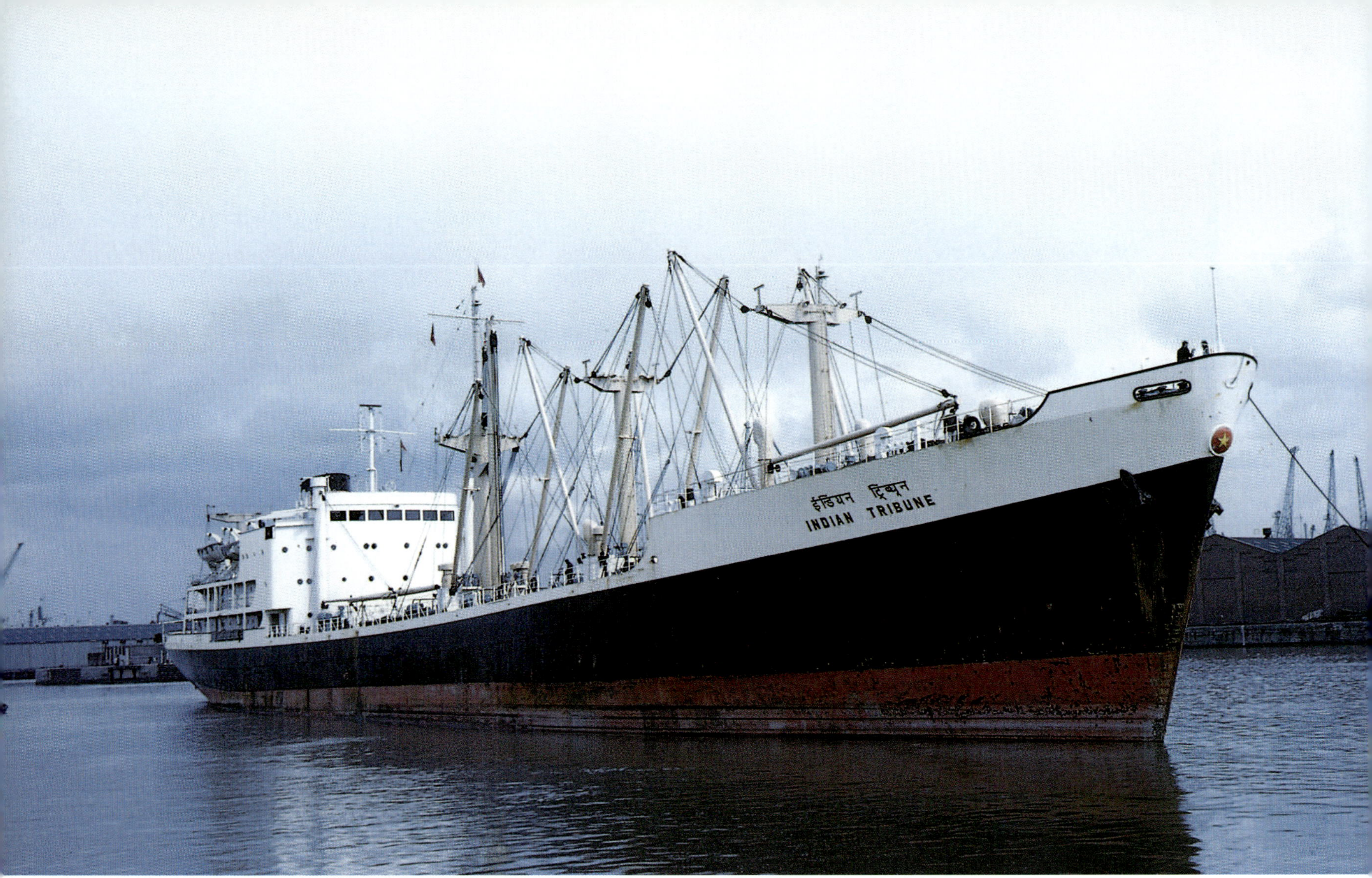

The ***Indian Tribune*** (IND, 8811grt/63) was photographed in Canada Dock, Liverpool, in 1970. She was built by the Greenock Dockyard Co Ltd as ***Clan Macgowan*** for the King Line Ltd and was launched on 14 December 1962. Following the completion of trials, ownership was transferred to The Clan Line Steamers Ltd to whom she was handed over in April 1963. In 1969 ownership reverted to the King Line and she was offered for sale. The following year she was acquired by the India Steamship Company and renamed ***Indian Tribune***. On 16 April 1979 she was hit amidships by the ***Bandar Abbas Express*** (SWE, 9074grt/78) while berthed at Bombay and was out of service for over six months. The ***Indian Tribune*** arrived at Calcutta on 24 May 1984 to be laid up and was eventually scrapped at that port in mid-1985.

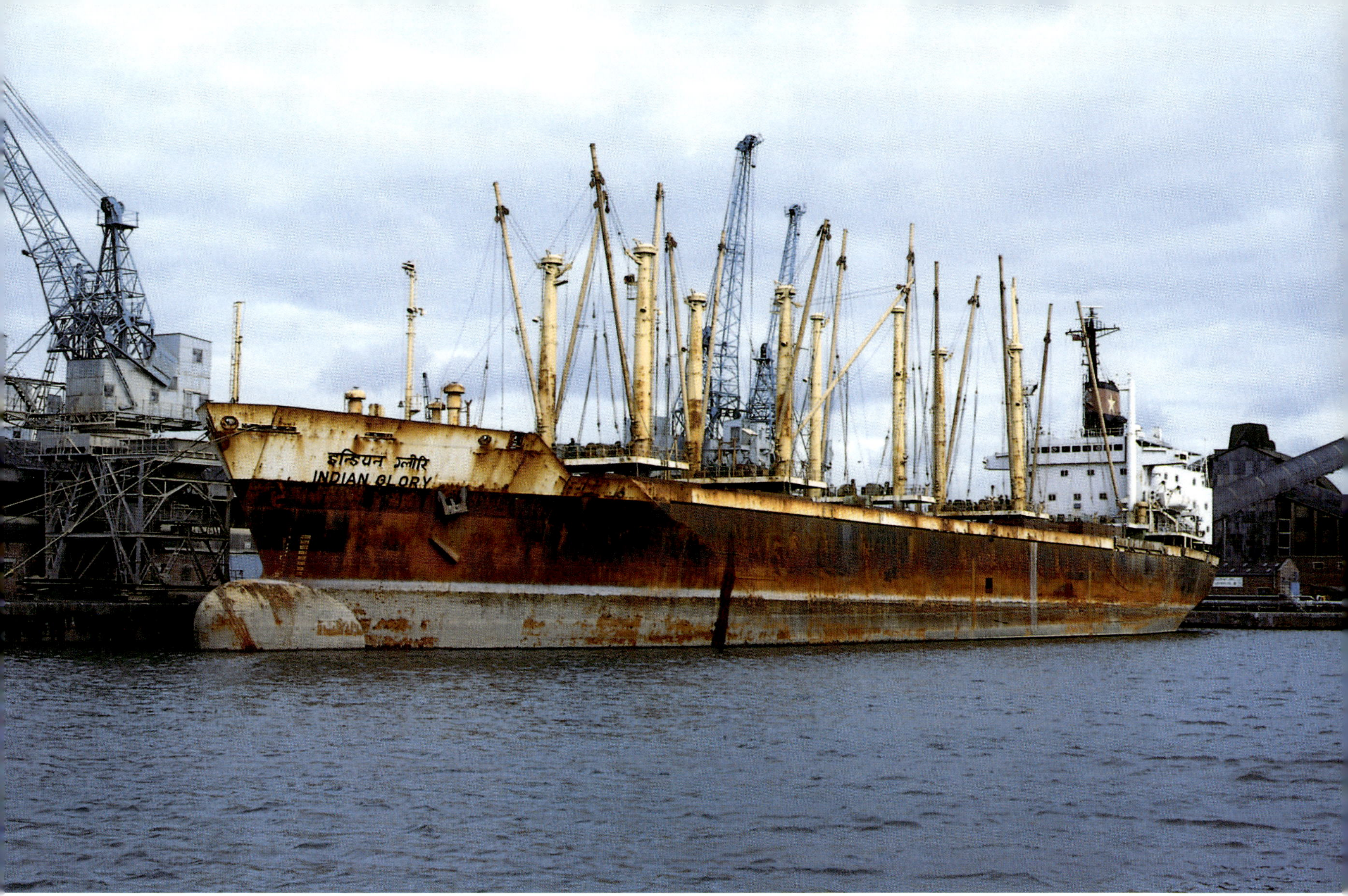

A rust-stained ***Indian Glory*** (IND, 13174grt/78) unloads at Berth 60 in Liverpool's Canada Branch Dock No. 1 in October 1984. She was built by the Hindustan Shipyard Ltd at Visakhapatnam in 1978 for the India Steamship Company. She is powered by an 18-cylinder Pielstick engine manufactured by Blohm & Voss in Hamburg. With her sixteen 10-ton derricks, she has been a very useful general cargo vessel. She became the Cypriot-flagged ***Trainer*** in February 1994, transferring to the Chinese flag and being renamed ***Hainan 3*** in July of that year and noted as trading in China. She was renamed ***Hai Nan No.1*** in 1995.

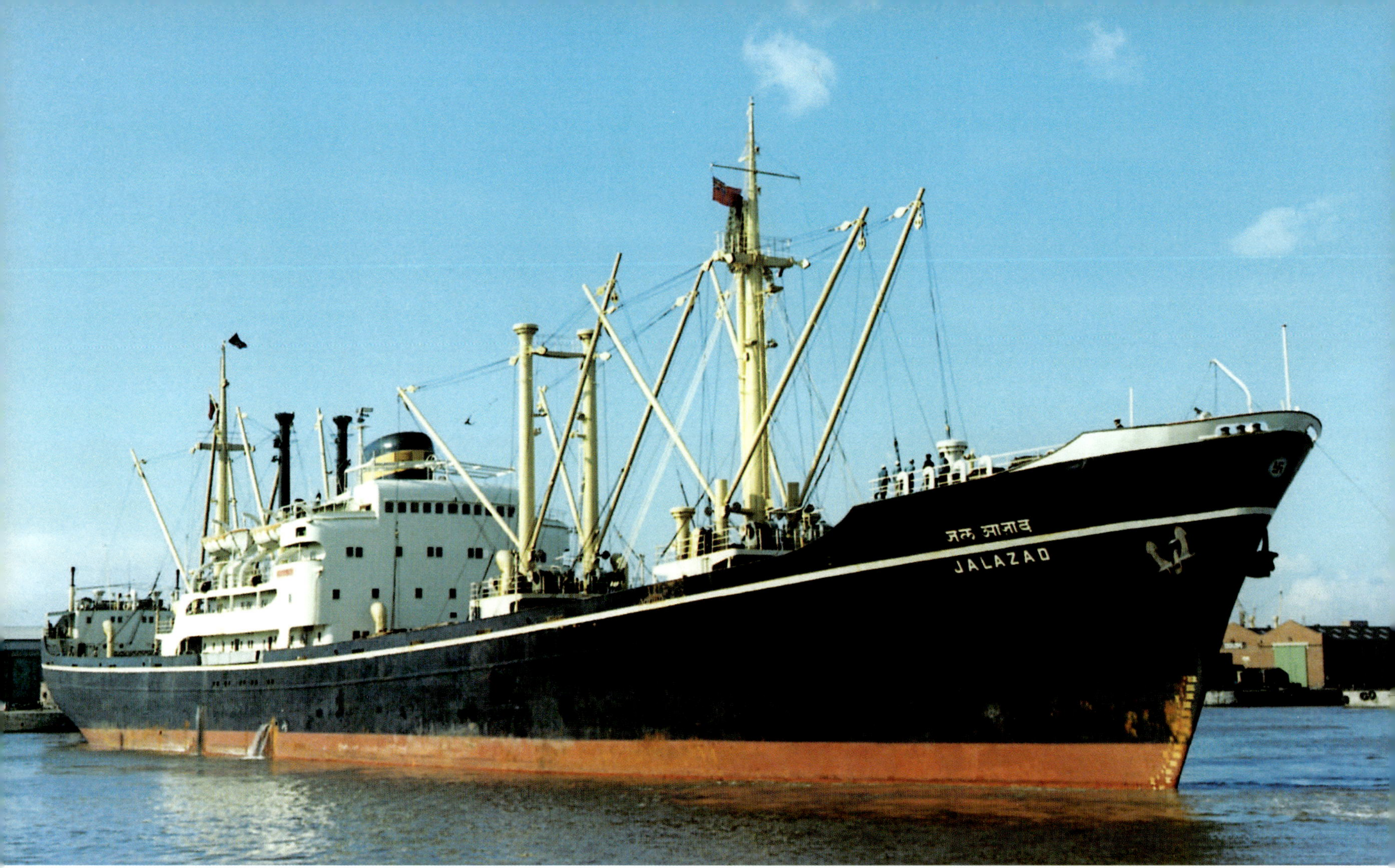

With the familiar “Jala” prefixes on their names, ships of the Scindia Steam Navigation Co Ltd were a common sight in the Mersey. Originally ships from this company and others based in the Indian sub-continent would have brought tea and raw materials for the Lancashire textile industry. However, by the 1960s, this industry was in decline and ironically the ships increasingly began to load export cargoes of machinery which served the rapidly-expanding domestic textile industry in their home countries. Powered by an 8-cylinder MAN engine, the ***Jalazad*** (IND, 6199grt/55) was built by the Lübecker Flender-Werke shipyard in Lübeck. She was launched on 18 March 1955 and completed two months later in May. She was a regular visitor to the Mersey, usually loading for Karachi and Bombay. In 1981, she was sold and renamed ***Jyoti Vinod*** but had only a very brief career as such. She was abandoned off Tema on 23 December 1981 and was eventually scuttled there in September 1983.

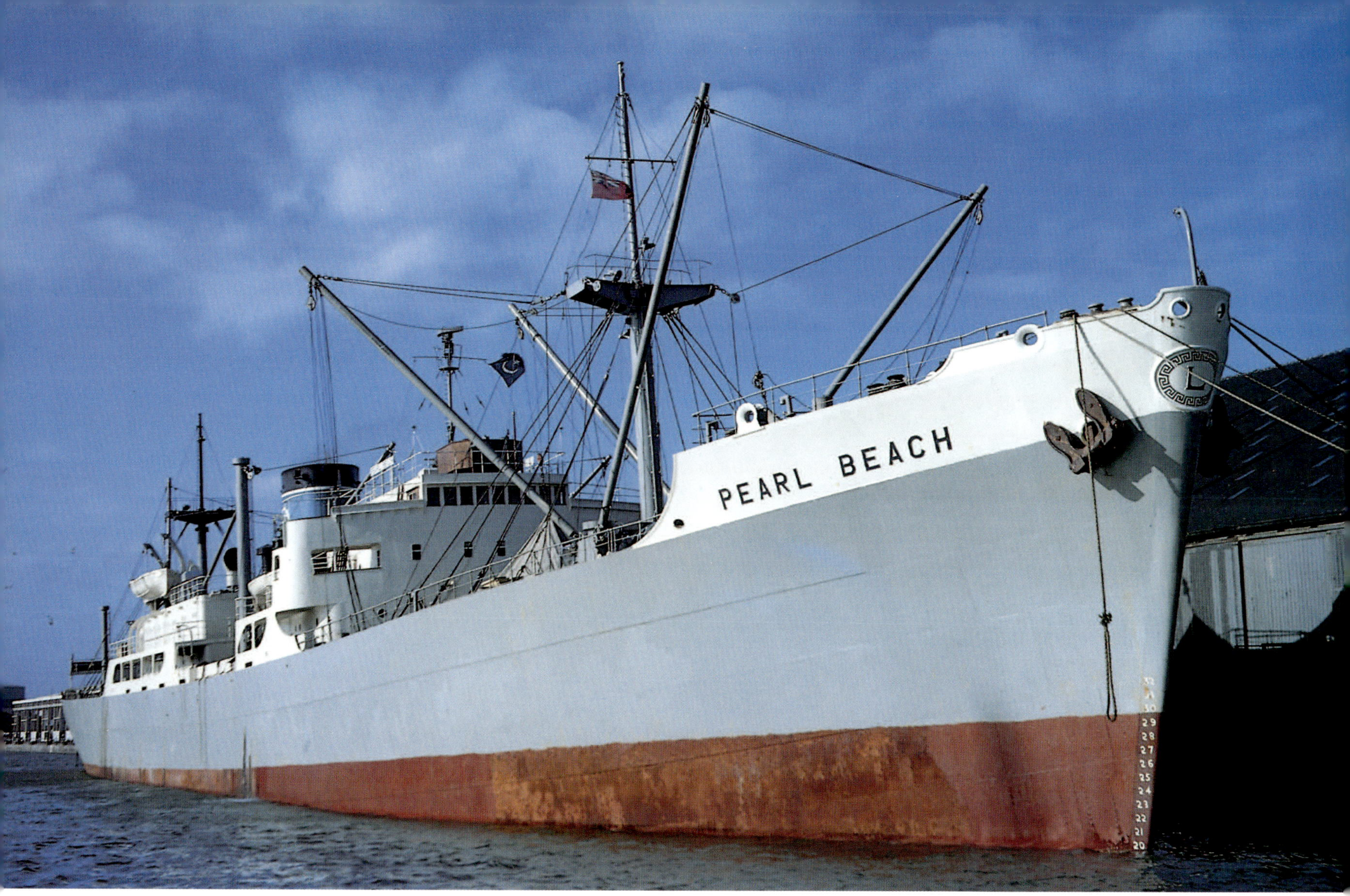

The ***Pearl Beach*** (LBR, 8692grt/58) is shown loading cargo at Berth 220 in the East Float at Birkenhead in late Summer 1968 when on charter to the National Shipping Corporation of Pakistan. She was built at the Wm Gray shipyard in West Hartlepool. Many of the cargo liners in this volume were bought by Liberian-flag operators after completion of their career under the Red Ensign. However, the Doxford-engined ***Pearl Beach*** and sistership ***Pearl Creek*** were built for the Monrovia Shipping Co Ltd, a Liberian company. Launched on 21 December 1957, she was completed in April 1958. She became ***Tarpon Swift*** in 1969, ***Taprobane Goodrich*** in 1977 and was broken up at Kaohsiung in 1979.

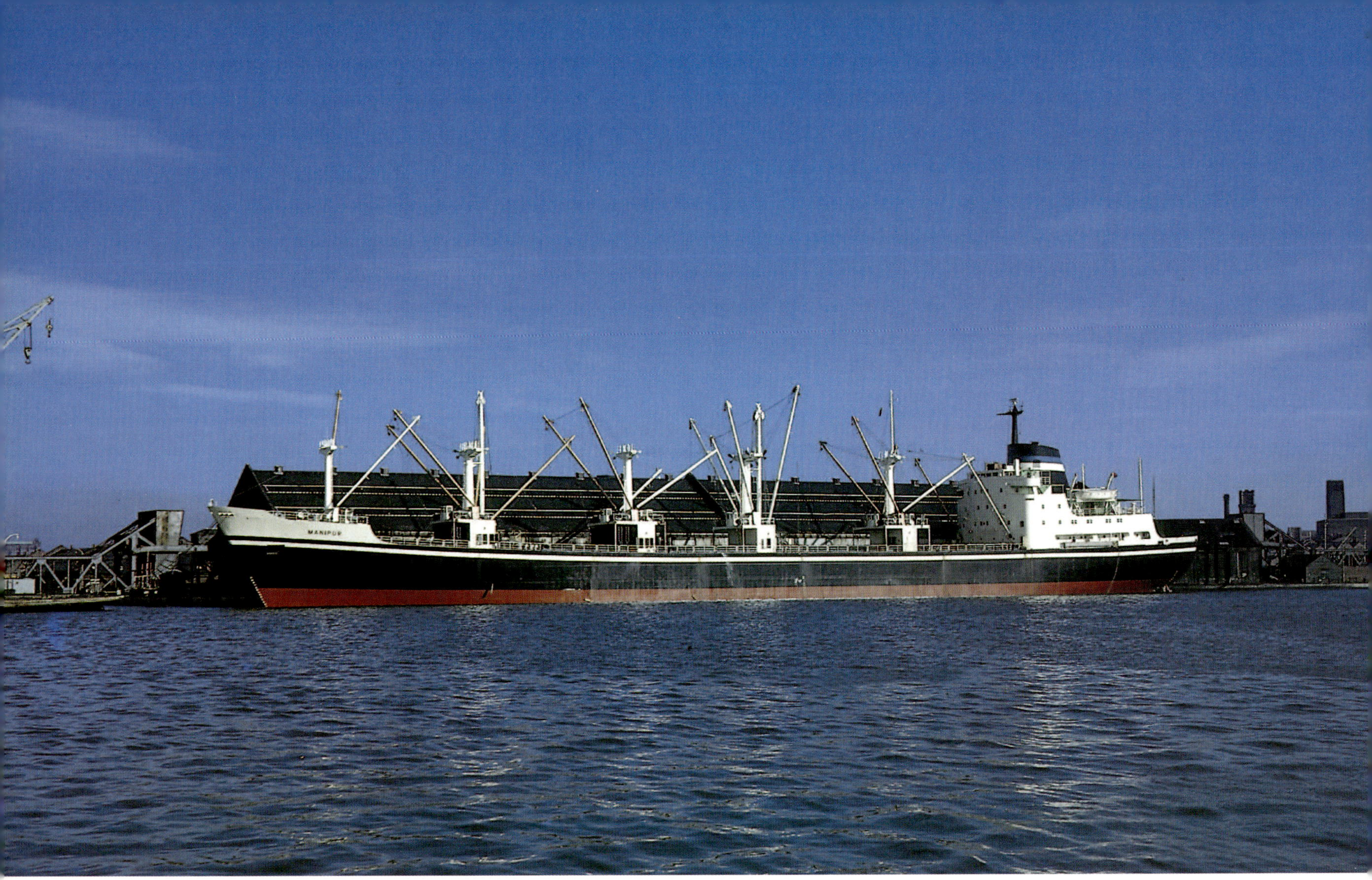

Another shipping company to have been long associated with the Mersey is the Brocklebank Line. Although the Brocklebank company had been owned by Cunard since 1919, the ships always retained their distinctive names and funnel colours. The ***Manipur*** (8783grt/64) was built at the Caledon shipyard in Dundee and was launched on 28 January 1964 with completion coming in September of that year. She was built as ***Ivernia*** for the Cunard Line and we have already seen her in Cunard colours on page 7. She was transferred to Brocklebank Line in 1970. In that same year, she was lengthened by some 24 metres, her gross tonnage increasing from 5149grt as built. Seen here in Spring 1971, she was briefly renamed ***Concordia Manipur*** for the duration of a charter in that same year. Sold by Brocklebank in 1977, she was sold to the expanding Mediterranean Shipping Company and was renamed ***Philippa***. She was eventually broken up at Chittagong where she arrived on 9 February 1985.

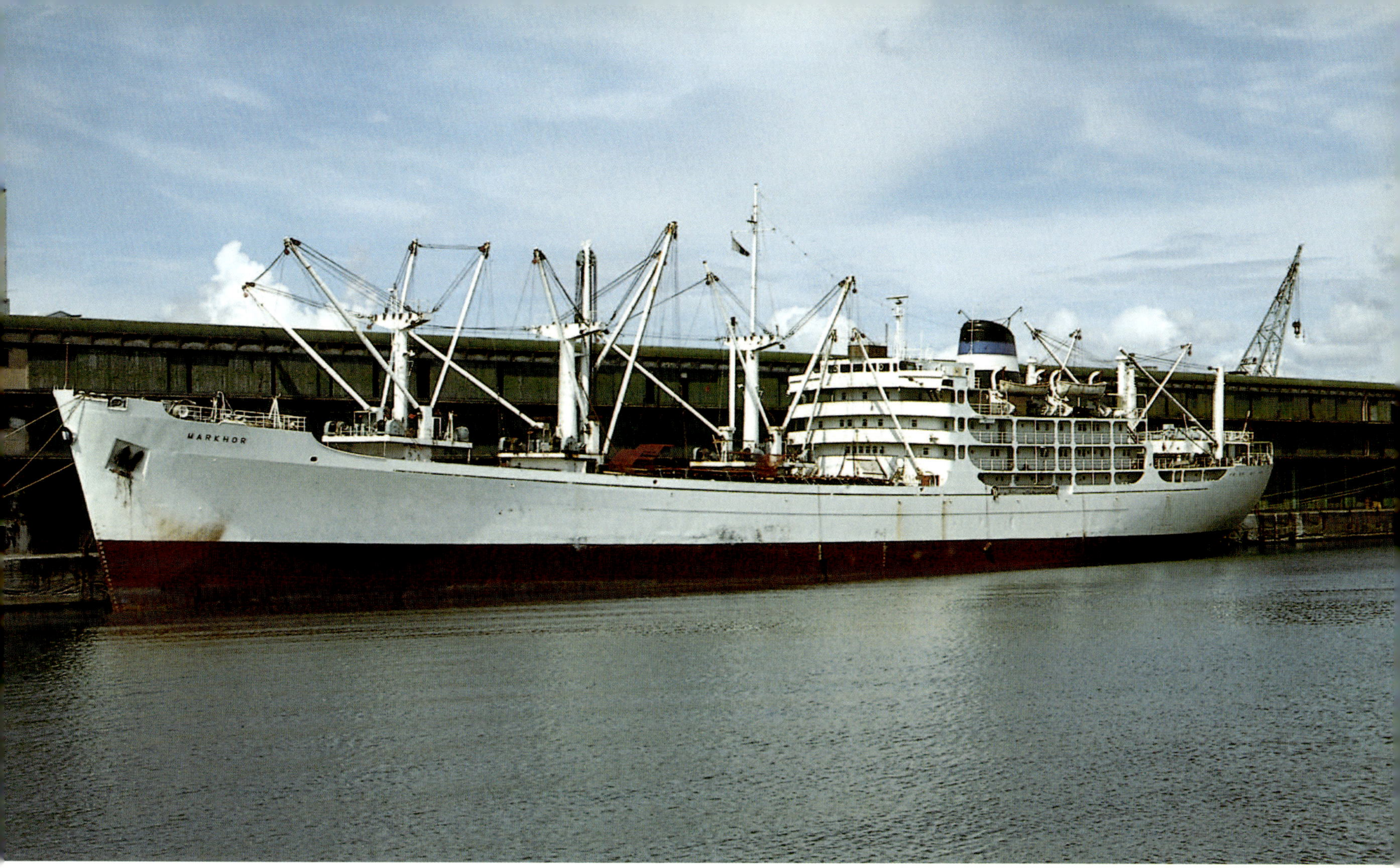

The Brocklebank company was started in Whitehaven by Thomas and John Brocklebank in 1801, originally to transport coal from the Cumbrian coalfield, and moved to Liverpool in 1819. In the 20th century, it was trading mainly to India but the development of containerisation and closure of the Suez Canal in the 1960s were largely responsible for the cessation of this trade. A new Cunard Brocklebank company was formed in 1967 to handle Cunard's cargo shipping interests. The ***Markhor*** (9120grt/63) was built by A Stephen & Sons Ltd at its Linthouse shipyard on the River Clyde. Powered by a 7-cylinder Sulzer engine, she was launched on 11 October 1962 and delivered in January 1963. The ***Markhor*** was sold and renamed ***Kara Unicorn*** in 1981 and was eventually scrapped at Dalian in China where she arrived on 1 June 1984. She originally had a black hull but when seen on 22 June 1980, this had been painted a distinctive white to reflect her ability to carry refrigerated cargoes. It is also worth noting that she was actually owned by Eggar, Forrester (Holdings) Ltd and bareboat chartered to Cunard Brocklebank. This was another method used by shipping companies to cope with the increasing financial problems faced in the 1960s and 1970s.

(Bernard McCall)

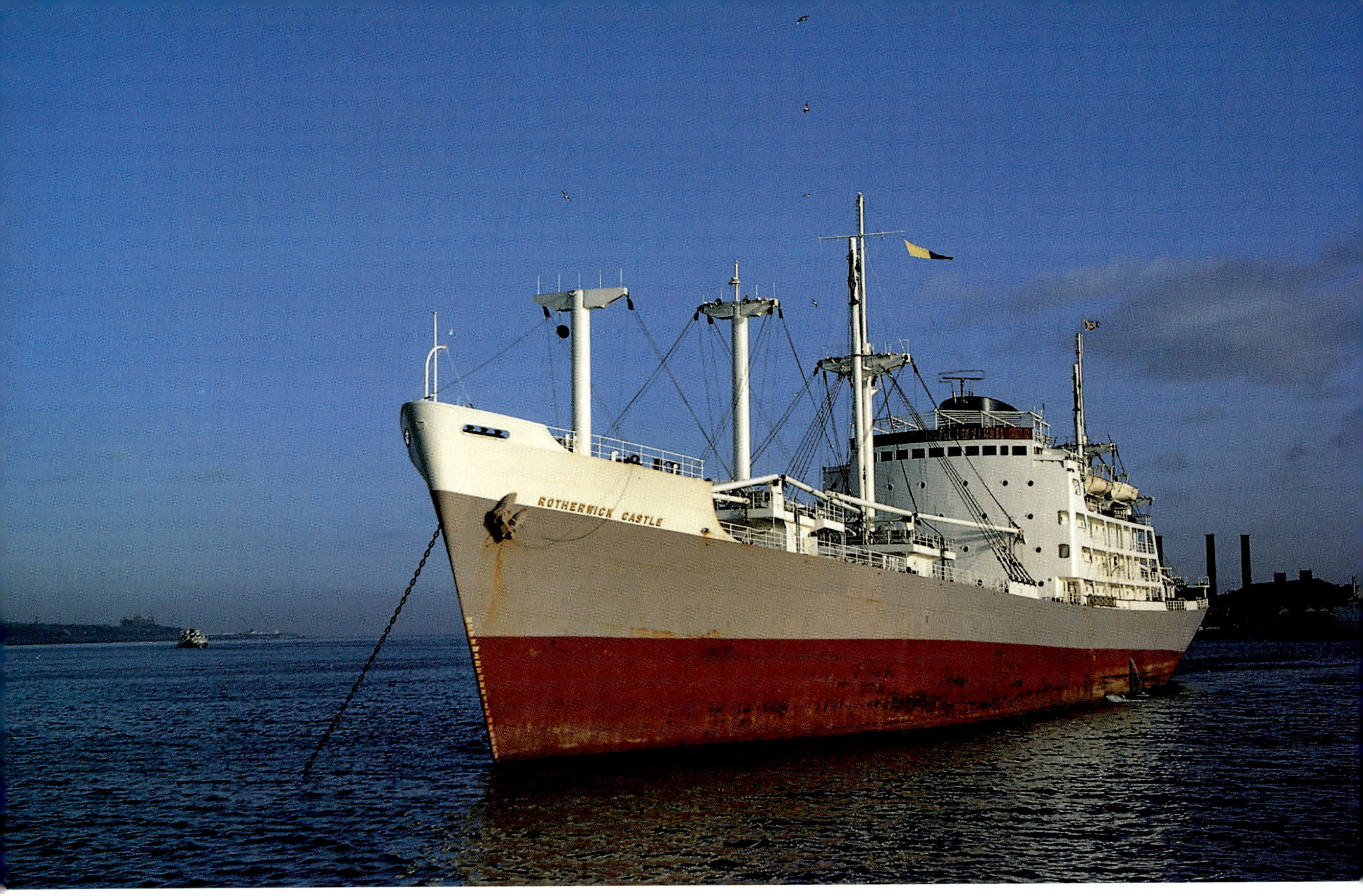

The ***Rotherwick Castle*** (9650grt/59) is anchored in the Mersey in Autumn 1968 waiting for tugs to take her to the Clan Line loading berth in Vittoria Dock, Birkenhead. She was built at the Cartsdyke East yard of the Greenock Dockyard Company and was launched on 19 August 1959, being completed and handed over to the Union Castle Line in December of that year. She and sistership ***Rothesay Castle*** were fast refrigerated vessels each fitted with a 6-cylinder B&W engine manufactured by J G Kincaid & Co Ltd and capable of 17 knots. The ships were designed to carry South African produce to the UK. She was sold in 1975 to Sea Fortune Shipping Company, Monrovia, and was renamed ***Sea Fortune***, later becoming ***Silver Rays*** in 1980 and was broken up at Chittagong in 1982.

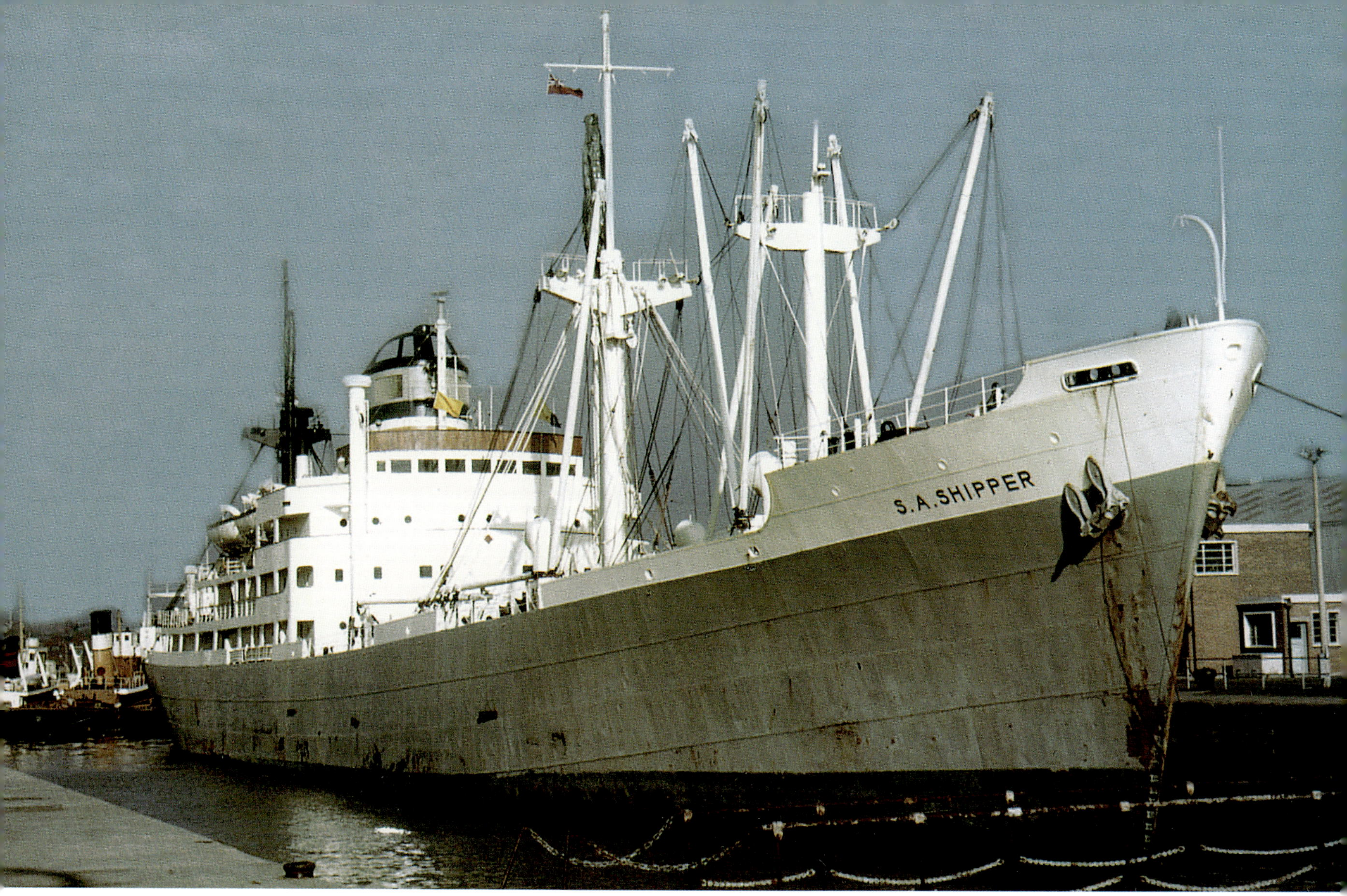

Safmarine's turbine steamer ***S.A.Shipper*** (ZAF, 7898grt/54) prepares to sail from Langton lock in Liverpool. She was built by the Greenock Dockyard in 1954 for the Clan Line and was launched on 17 March 1954. Named ***Clan Robertson,*** she was handed over on 18 June. Her ownership was transferred to Bullard, King & Company in early 1959 and she was given the name ***Umzinto*** later in the year. She was transferred to Springbok Line in 1960 and renamed ***Rooibok***, later becoming ***South African Shipper*** in 1961 when her owners were taken over by the South African Marine Corporation Ltd (Safmarine). Her name was abbreviated to ***S. A. Shipper*** in 1966 and she was broken up at Kaohsiung where she arrived on 26 November 1975, demolition starting one month later.

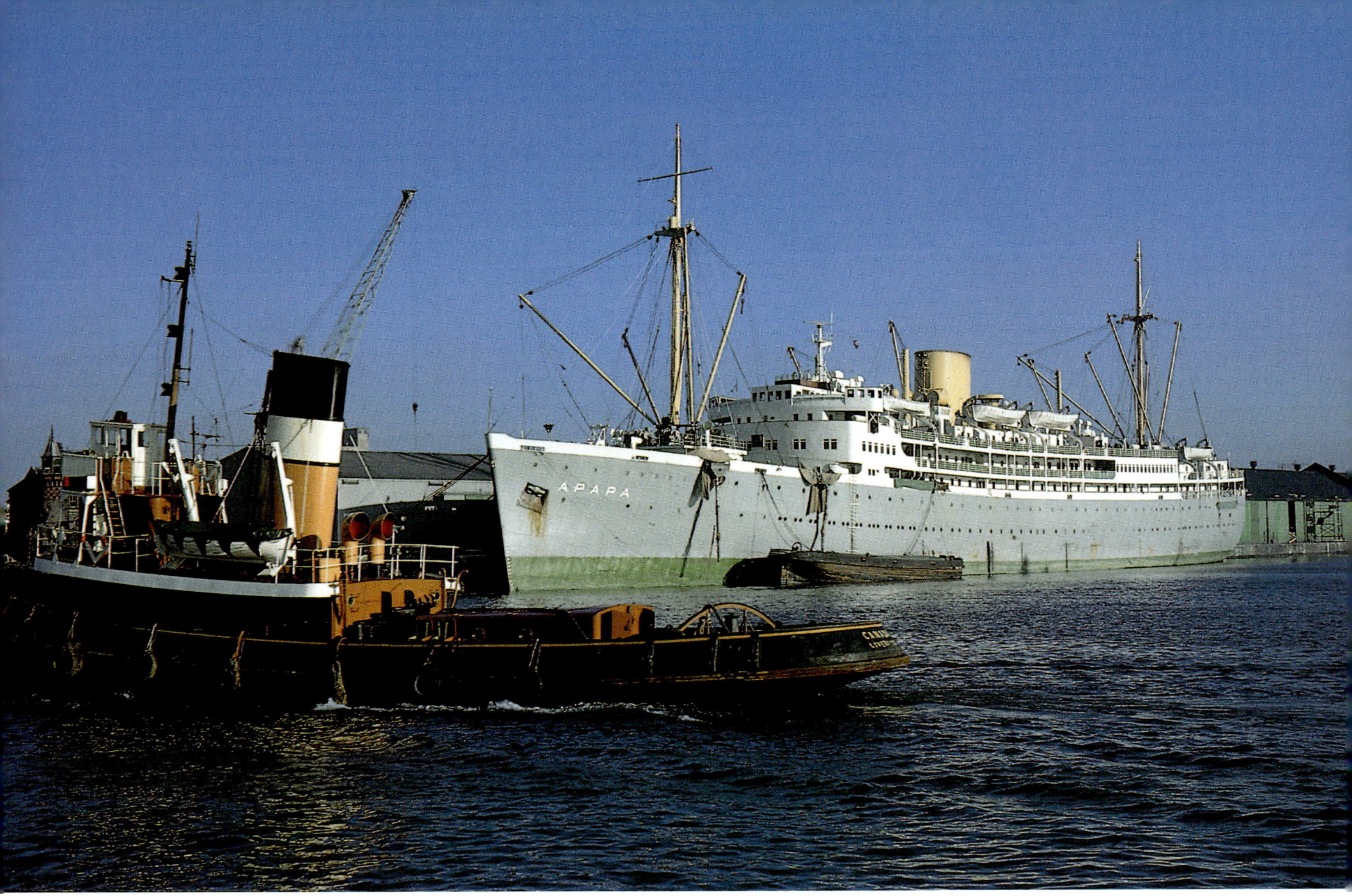

Elder Dempster Line's ***Apapa*** (11651grt/48) is seen at Berth 73 in Brocklebank Dock in 1968 before departing on her 177th and final sailing to West Africa on 20 September. She was later sold to Shun Cheong Steam Navigation Company, Hong Kong, for service from Hong Kong to Singapore and Penang. She was renamed ***Taipooshan*** retaining Liverpool as her port of registry and operated on this service until 1975 when she was sold and broken up at Kaohsiung, arriving there on 23 February 1975. She had been built at the Vickers-Armstrong shipyard in Barrow and was launched on 18 August 1947. She was handed over to Elder Dempster in March 1948.

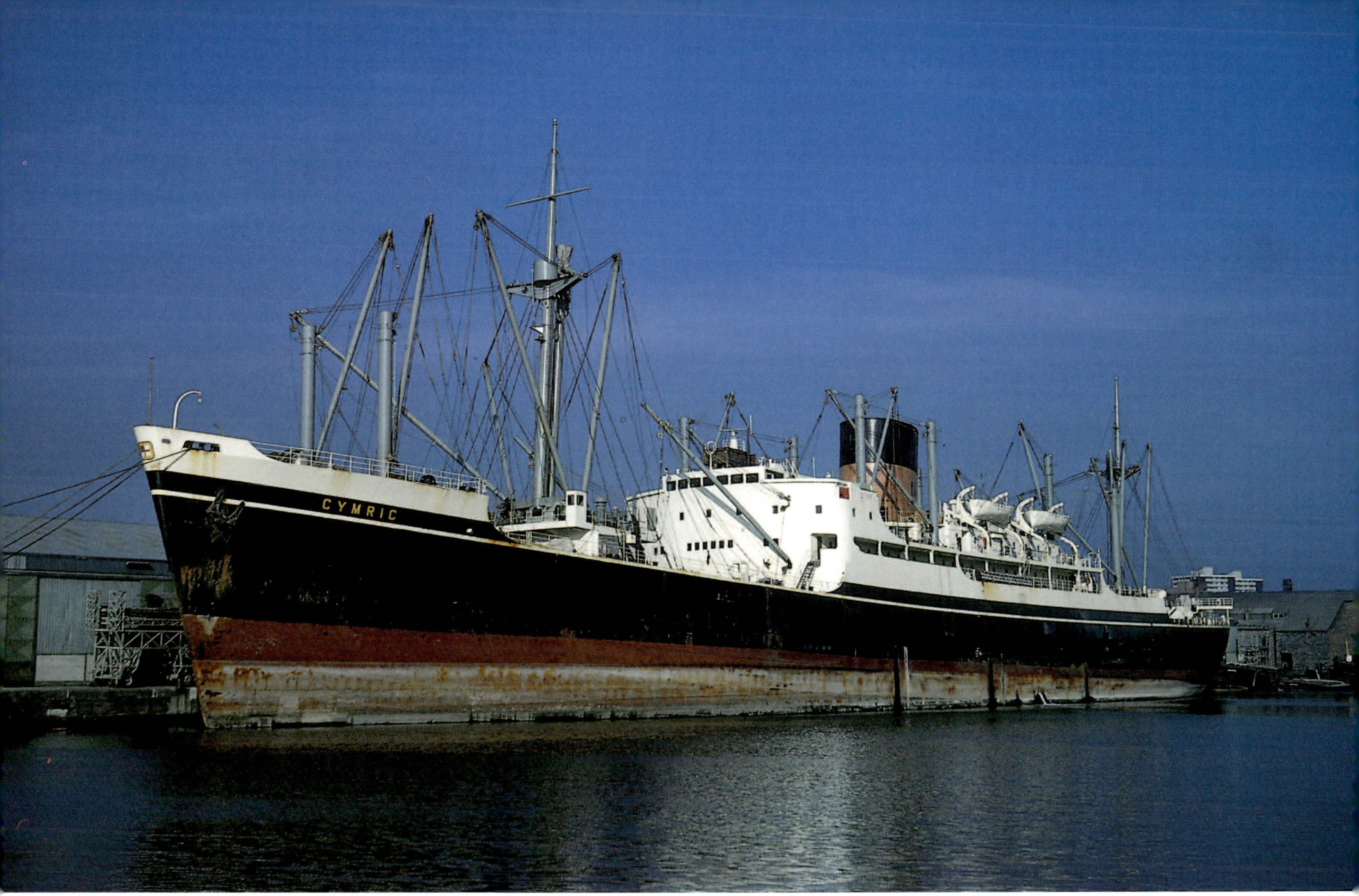

Shaw, Savill & Albion Line's ***Cymric*** (10916grt/53) was built by Harland & Wolff at Belfast. Launched on 5 November 1952, she was handed over on 15 May 1953. She was powered by two 6-cylinder B&W engines manufactured by her builder and these gave her a speed of 17 knots. She was the second of five near-identical refrigerated ships built for her owner's service from Australia to the UK. Like the other four vessels, she had almost 334,000 cubic feet of refrigerated space and also had a 70-ton derrick. Though still remaining in Shaw Savill ownership, she was transferred to Royal Mail Line management in 1972 and was renamed ***Durango***. She was yet another vessel to meet her end at Kaohsiung where she arrived for demolition on 18 October 1975.

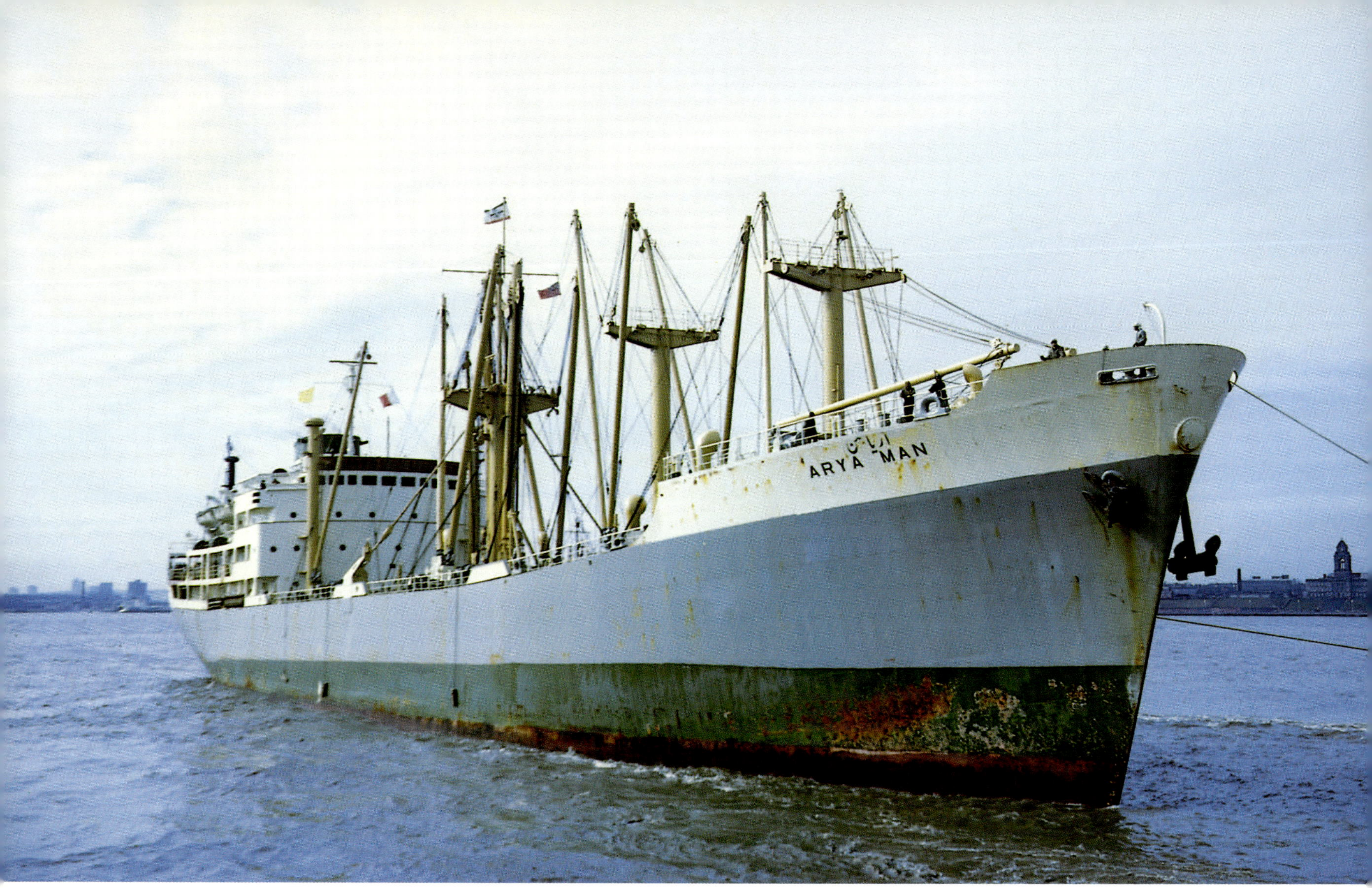

Arya National Shipping Lines of Iran cargo vessel ***Arya Man*** (DEU, 9240grt/61) was photographed in the Mersey off Langton Dock in Spring 1970. She was built in 1961 as ***Clan Forbes*** for the Clan Line Steamers Ltd. Not a product of the Greenock Dockyard Company like other Clan Line ships we have seen so far in this volume, she was built at Wallsend on the River Tyne by Swan, Hunter & Wigham Richardson. She was launched on 2 March 1961 and handed over to Clan Line in June of that year. Sold in 1968, she became ***Arya Man***. Some sources suggest Iranian ownership but *Lloyd's Register* lists her owners as a German company based in Lübeck. In 1980, she was certainly bought by Iranian interests, becoming ***Iran Hemmet***. She was broken up at Alang in 1986, having arrived there on 3 October 1985.

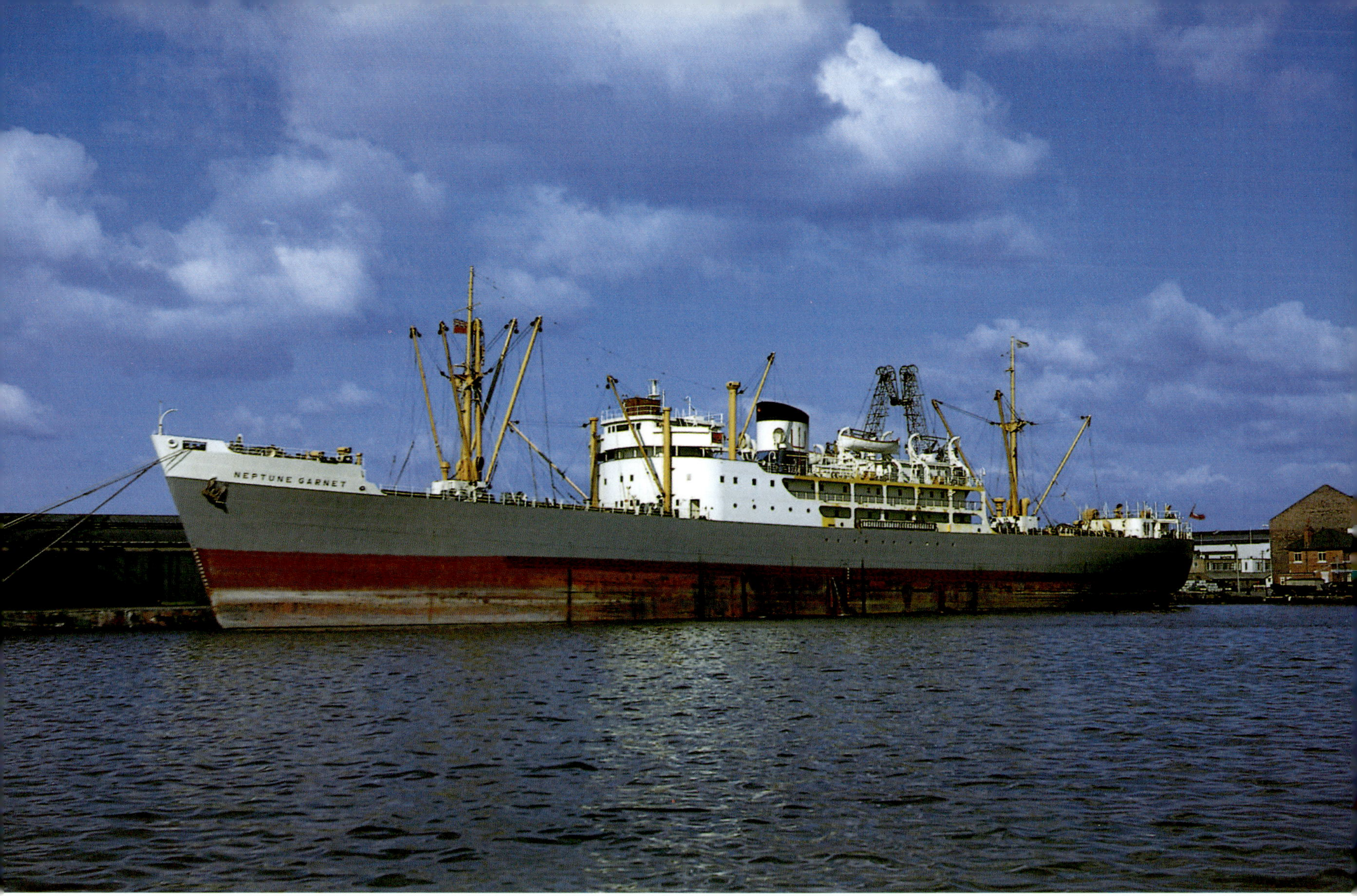

The ***Neptune Garnet*** (SGP, 7791grt/56) was photographed at Berth 222 in the West Float, Birkenhead, in 1973. She had recently been purchased by the Neptune Orient Lines, Singapore, from the Royal Mail Lines. She was built by Harland & Wolff at Belfast as the ***Eden*** and was powered by a 2-stroke 6-cylinder engine manufactured by her builder. She was launched on 19 October 1955 and handed over to Royal Mail Lines on 1 February 1956. She survived in service until 1979 when she was broken up at Kaohsiung.

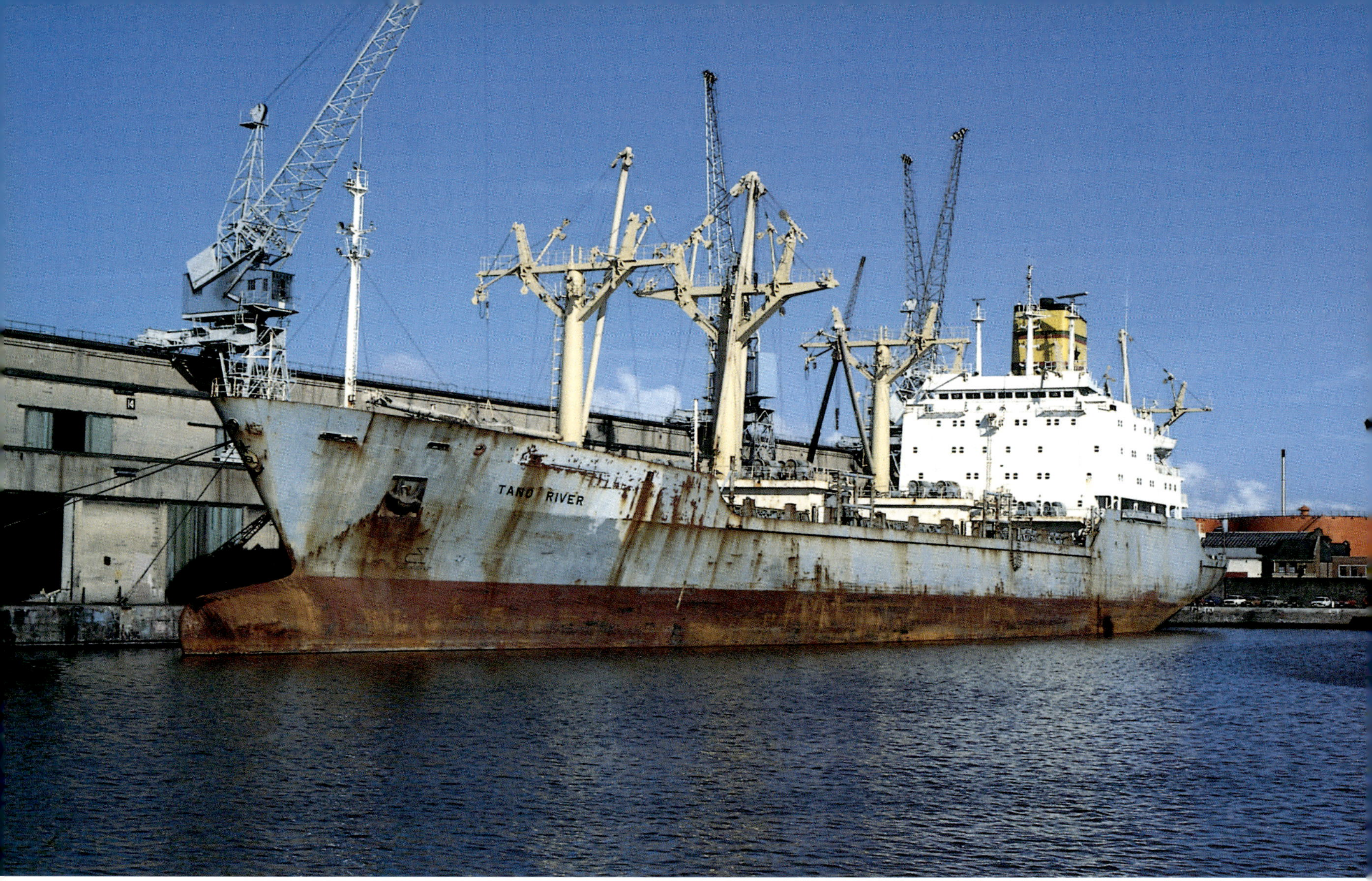

By the late 1970s, shipyards in the Far East were rapidly expanding in stark contrast to yards in northern Europe. The Black Star Line's ***Tano River*** (GHA, 13004grt/80), loading at Berth 54 in Huskisson Branch Dock No. 1 in Autumn 1984, was built at the Hyundai yard in Ulsan. Launched on 15 August 1979, she was completed in February of the following year. She was sold to Cypriot interests in 1994 and renamed ***Verano***. In 1999 she was repossessed by the First National Bank following her arrest whilst laid up at Falmouth. She was sold later that year to optimistically-named Profit Shipping Co Ltd, Cyprus, renamed ***Express Hyphestos*** and was beached for demolition at Mumbai on 24 June 2002.

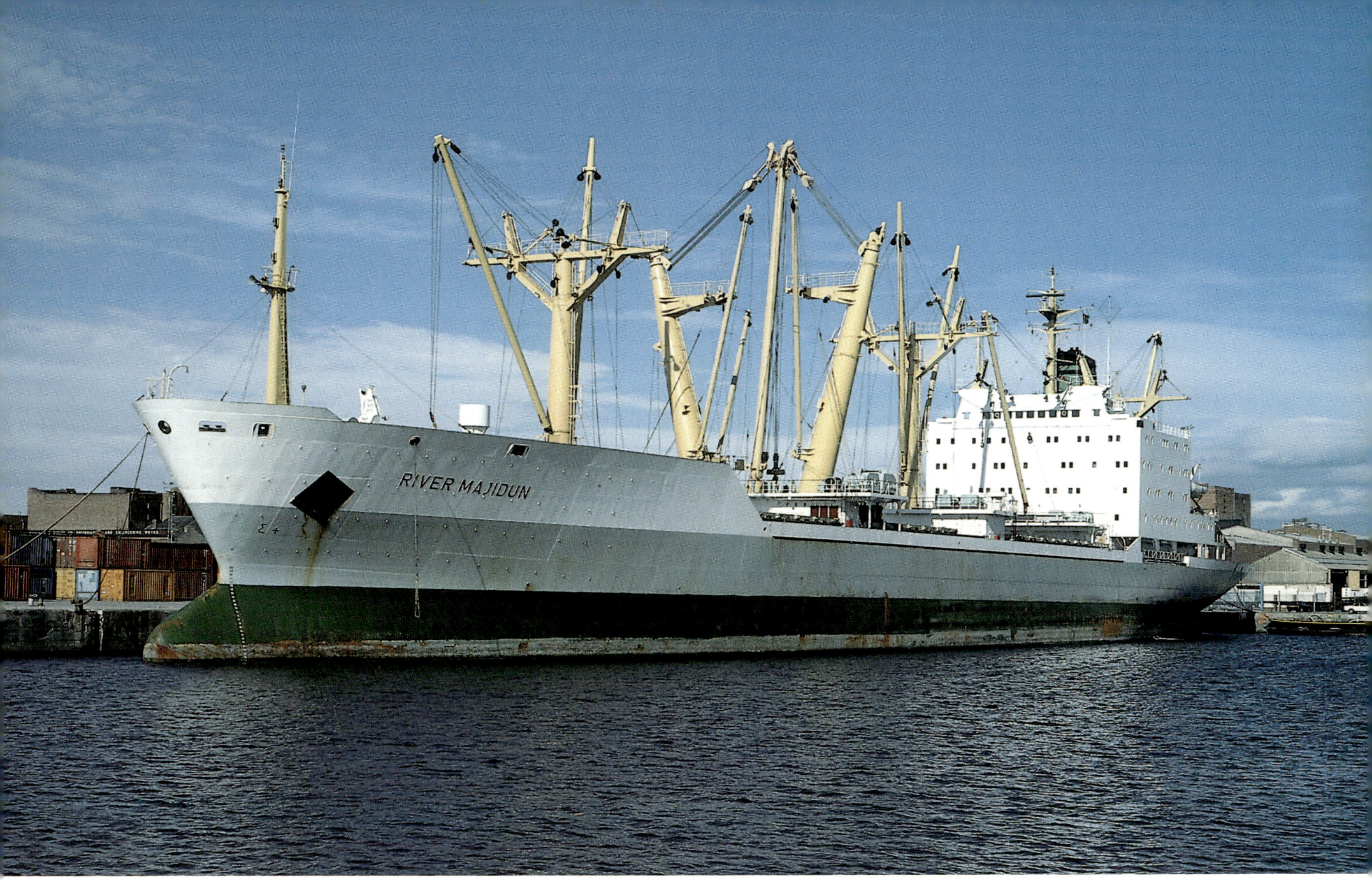

Not only was competition coming from shipyards in the Far East but also from those in central Europe where, again, labour costs were much lower than in northern Europe. The ***River Majidun*** (NGA, 13161grt/79) was built at the Brodogradiliste shipyard in Split. She was launched on 31 March 1979, completed in December of that year and was operated by the Nigerian National Shipping Line on its services from European ports to West Africa. She arrived at anchorage off Las Palmas on 7 March 1994 and went aground the following month on 3 April. She was subsequently towed to sea and scuttled. With the owning company in financial difficulties in the mid-1990s, its ships were laid up and arrested including some on Merseyside. The ***River Majidun*** is seen here at Berth 63 in Canada Branch Dock No. 3 in late Summer 1985.

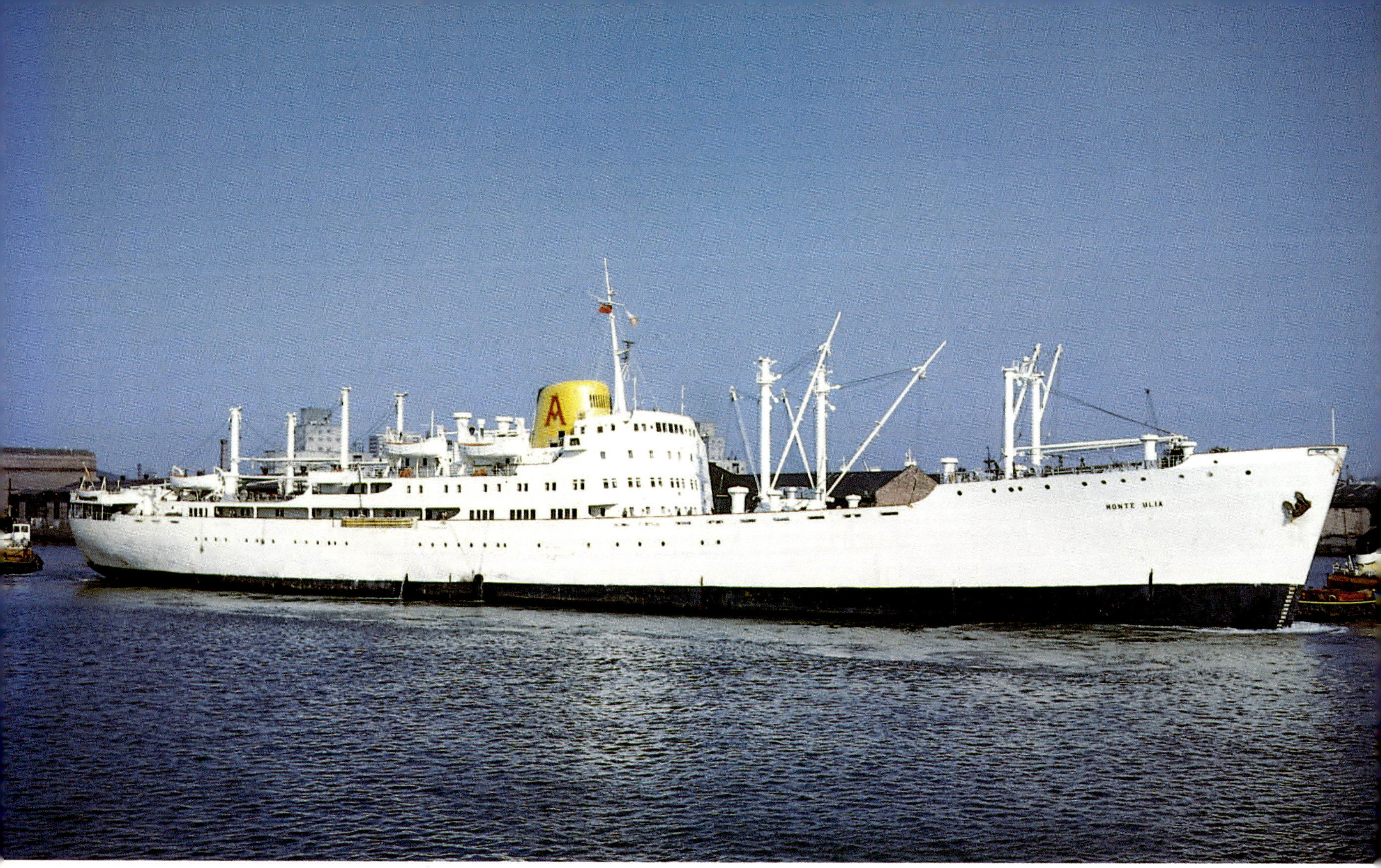

The white ships of Spanish company Naviera Aznar were a regular sight in the Mersey. The company's main service was from Spanish ports to South America but its ships also linked Liverpool and London to the Canary Islands. The ***Monte Ulia*** (ESP, 10123grt/52) was built at the Astilleros Españoles shipyard in Sestao, near Bilbao, and was the last of four cargo/passenger ships ordered by the Spanish government in the late 1940s. Able to carry 74 passengers, she was completed in March 1952. In this photograph, we see her swinging in Alexandra No. 3 Dock on 6 May 1975. She made her final passenger-carrying voyage in September 1975 and a plan to continue to use her as a freight-only vessel seems not to have materialised. She was sold and renamed ***Climax Opal*** in 1976. Already having suffered a fire whilst under repair at Sestao in October 1975, she suffered a further serious fire in Belfast on 2 April 1977 and was sold for demolition in Santander where she arrived on 7 June 1977.

(C J Tabarin)

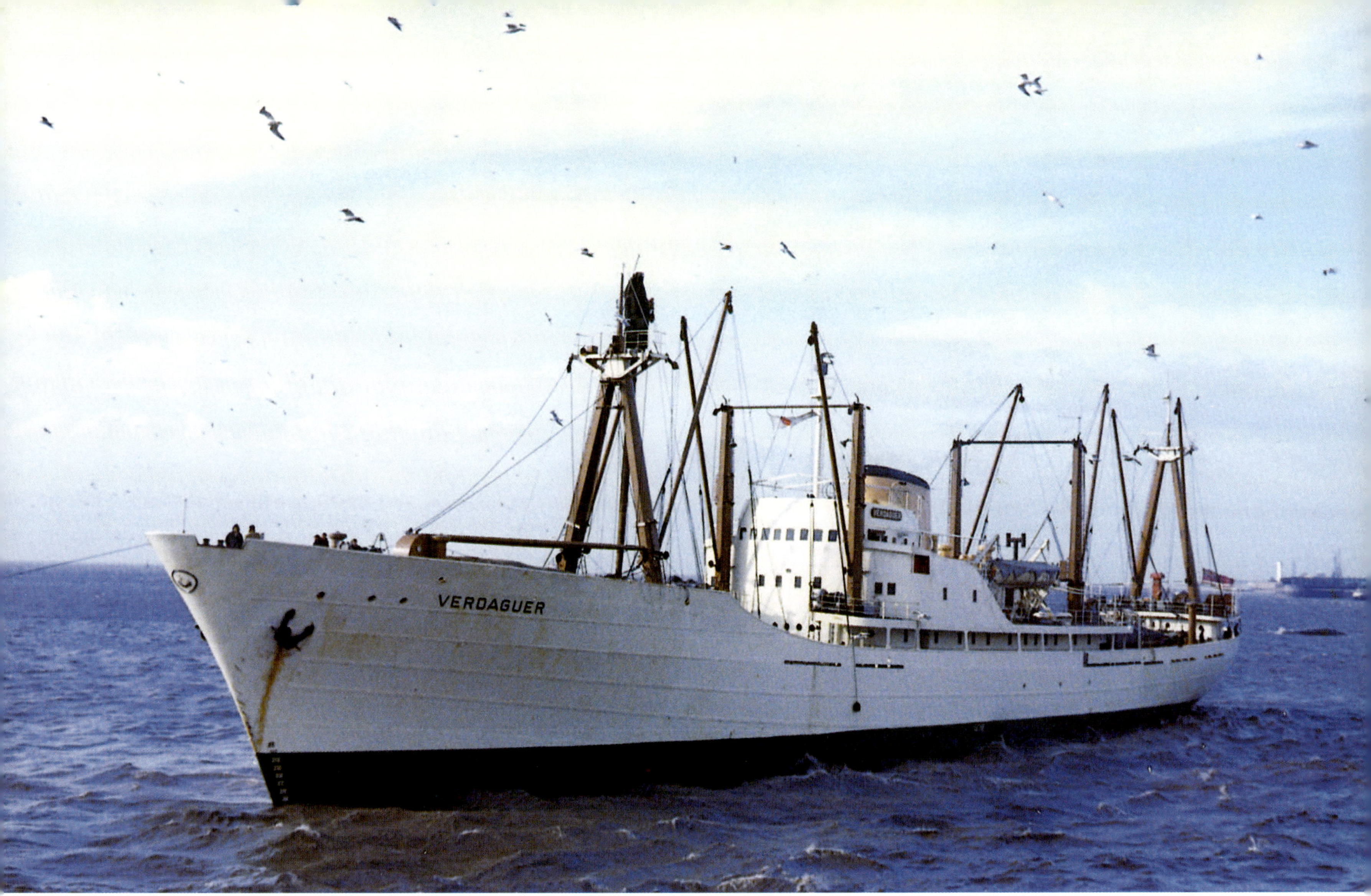

The ***Verdaguer*** (2049grt/58) of the MacAndrew Line arrives in the River Mersey at the end of a voyage from Spanish ports in 1967. She was built at the Krögerwerft shipyard in Schacht-Audorf on the bank of the Kiel Canal just east of Rendsburg. Powered by two 10-cylinder MAN engines, she was launched on 18 January 1958 and was completed in May of that year and traded from Liverpool to the Iberian peninsula until she was sold in 1971 to a Panamanian-flag operator by whom she was renamed ***Ursa***. She was broken up at Alang in 1992 having arrived there on 26 December 1991. In its advertising material during the 1960s, the MacAndrew Line boasted that it had served Spain for over two centuries.

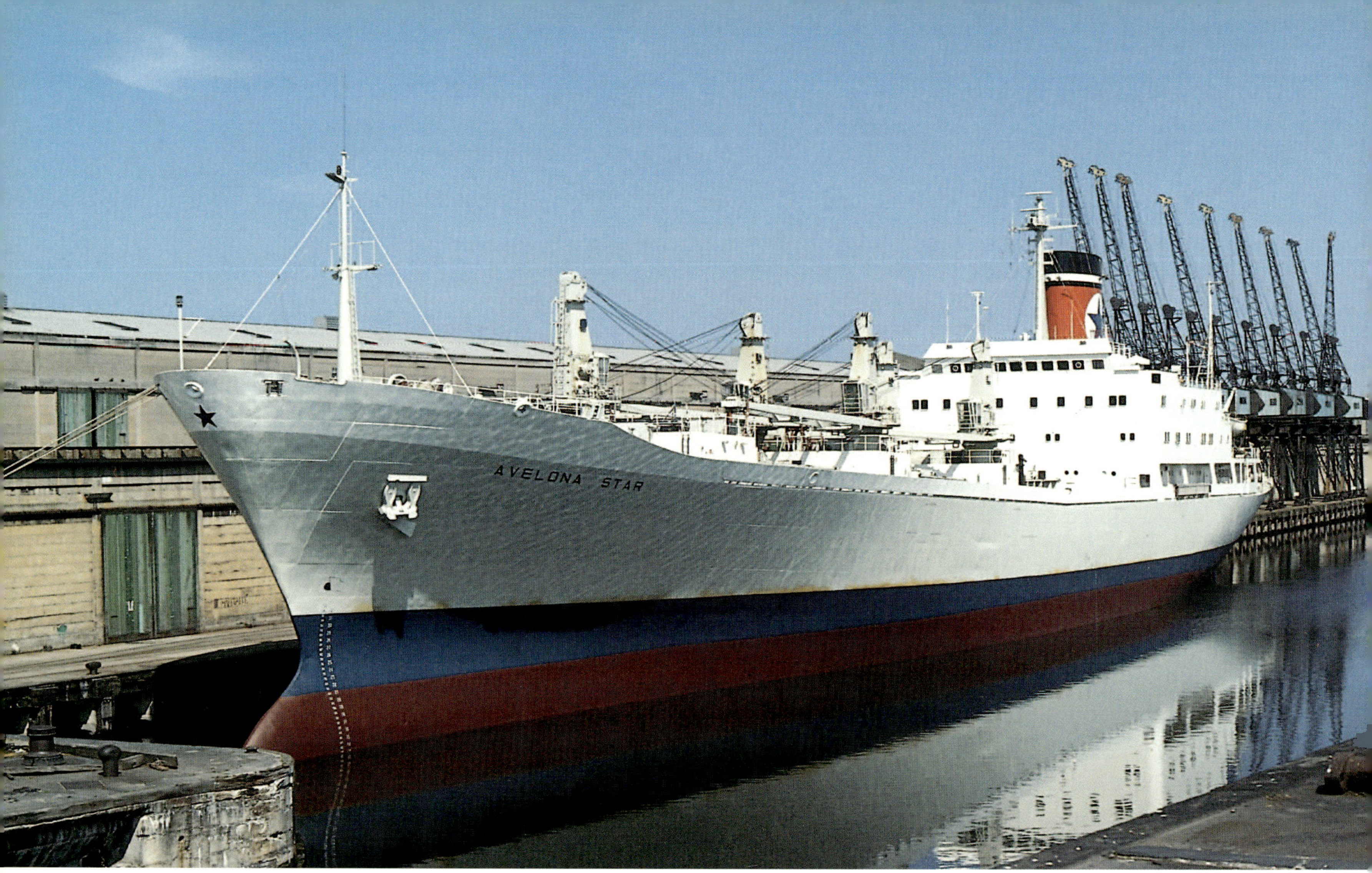

The ***Avelona Star*** (9784grt/75) was built by Smith's Dock at Middlesbrough for the Blue Star Line. She was launched on 12 May 1975 and delivered in December of that year. She was chartered by the UK government for service as a general supply during the Falklands campaign in 1982. She is seen here in early 1984. Sold in 1985, she was renamed ***Castle Peak*** and was chartered back to Blue Star. In 1988, she became ***Avelona Star*** once again, then ***Hornsound*** and ***Avelona Star*** in 1990. On 15 March of that year, she grounded in the River Scheldt off Terneuzen and was refloated undamaged the following day. In 2001, she was sold and renamed ***Baltic Wind*** and continues to trade as such in mid-2007. She is seen here at Berth 58 in Canada Dock West.

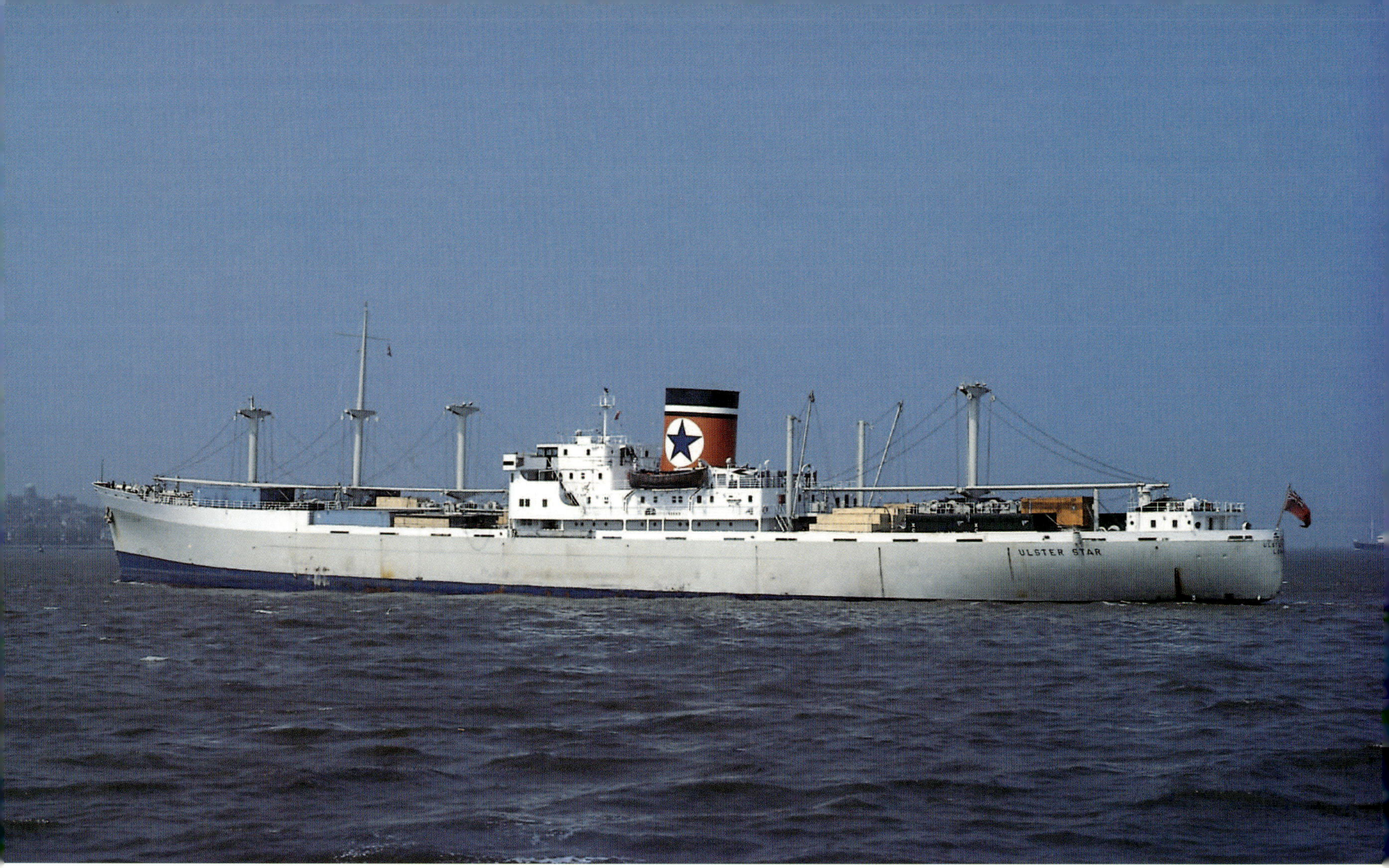

The ***Ulster Star*** (10413grt/59), photographed as she left Langton Lock on 22 May 1978, was a product of the Harland & Wolff shipyard in Belfast. Launched on 26 February 1959, she was handed over to Blue Star Line Ltd on 3 July and placed on the company's service to Australia. In 1972, she was transferred to the South America service after Blue Star withdrew its passenger-carrying ships from that route. She remained with the company throughout her life although in 1964 ownership was transferred to Lamport and Holt and she was bareboat chartered to Blue Star. Ownership reverted to Blue Star the following year. Her two-stroke double acting B&W engine was less than popular with her engineers. With three pistons in each cylinder unit, they had an over-abundance of working parts; "a piece of Victorian engineering somehow transmuted into the 20th century" was one comment. Like many ships of her style and generation, she was sold for demolition in Kaohsiung where she arrived on 13 August 1979 with work commencing on 3 October 1979.

(C J Tabarin)

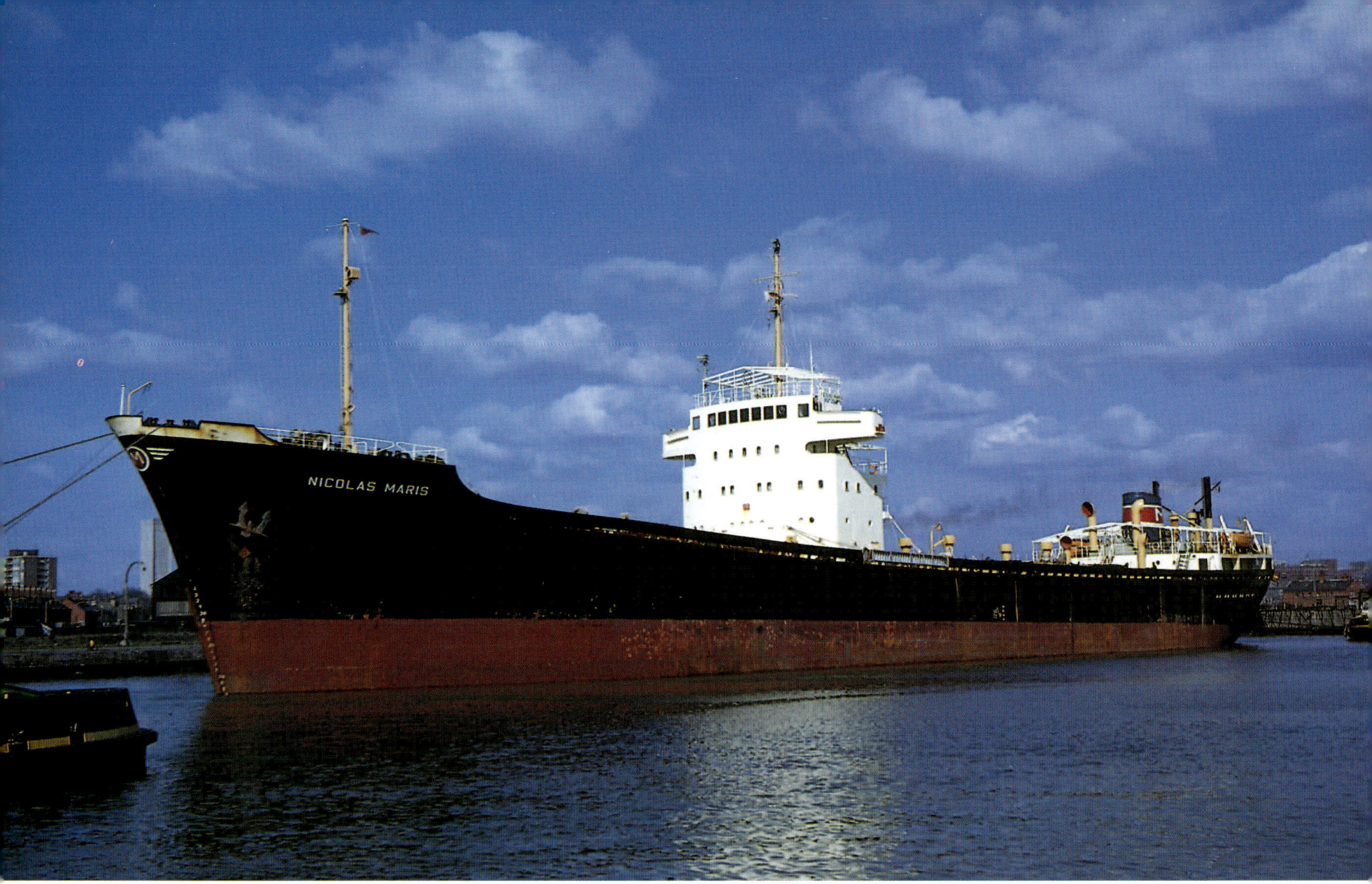

The bulk carrier ***Nicolas Maris*** (LBR, 7324grt/58) was built as ***Kreeft*** at the De Hoop shipyard in Lobith. Launched on 12 October 1957, she was completed in January of the following year. She became ***Nicolas Maris*** in 1965. She was involved in a serious collision with the ***Ivan Sechenov*** (RUS, 5626grt/56) in the Sea of Marmara on 12 January 1977. Sadly, 22 crew members of the Russian ship lost their lives. Two years later, she was sold to Afovos Maritime S.A. and renamed ***Afovos***. Another sale saw her become ***Miki*** in 1981. Her later career is mysterious. Some sources suggest she was renamed ***Eubal*** in 1982, reverting to ***Miki*** in 1983. This is not noted in *Lloyd's Register*. Movement reports suggest she left Haifa on 24 May 1982 but nothing further is heard of her under any name. She is reported by one source to have been scrapped at Aliaga in 1988. Here she is seen in Alfred Dock, Birkenhead, in Summer 1973.

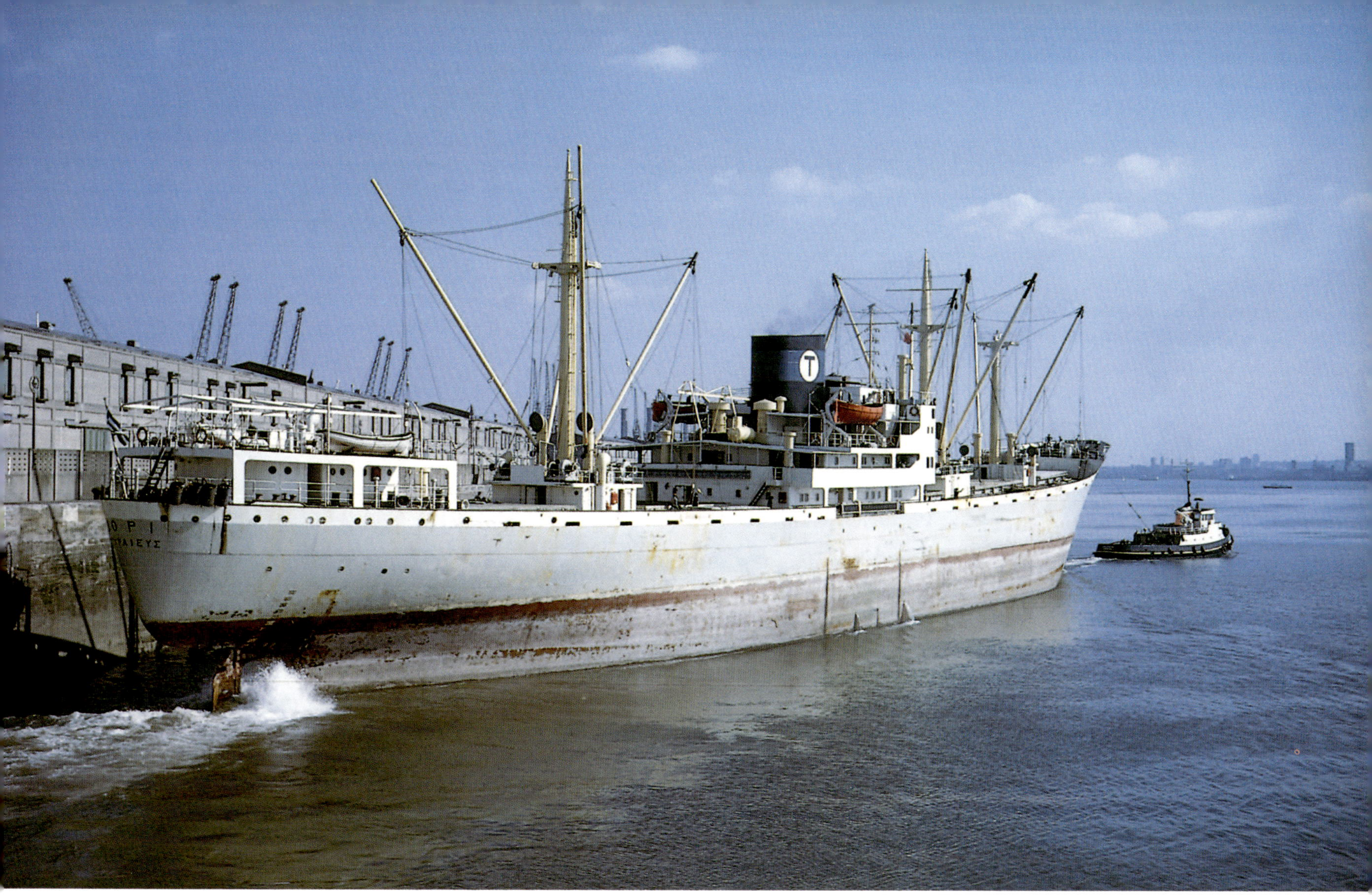

Outward bound from Langton lock on 6 May 1975 is the ***Vori*** (GRC, 7727grt/57). Powered by a 6-cylinder B&W engine, she was built by Nakskov Skibsværft and was launched on 21 March 1957 as ***Tasmania*** for Danish owners. In 1973, she was sold to Greek owners and renamed ***Vori***. She suffered a fire when off Abidjan on 4 September 1978 and was eventually sold to Spanish shipbreakers, arriving at Bilbao in late June 1979.

(C J Tabarin)

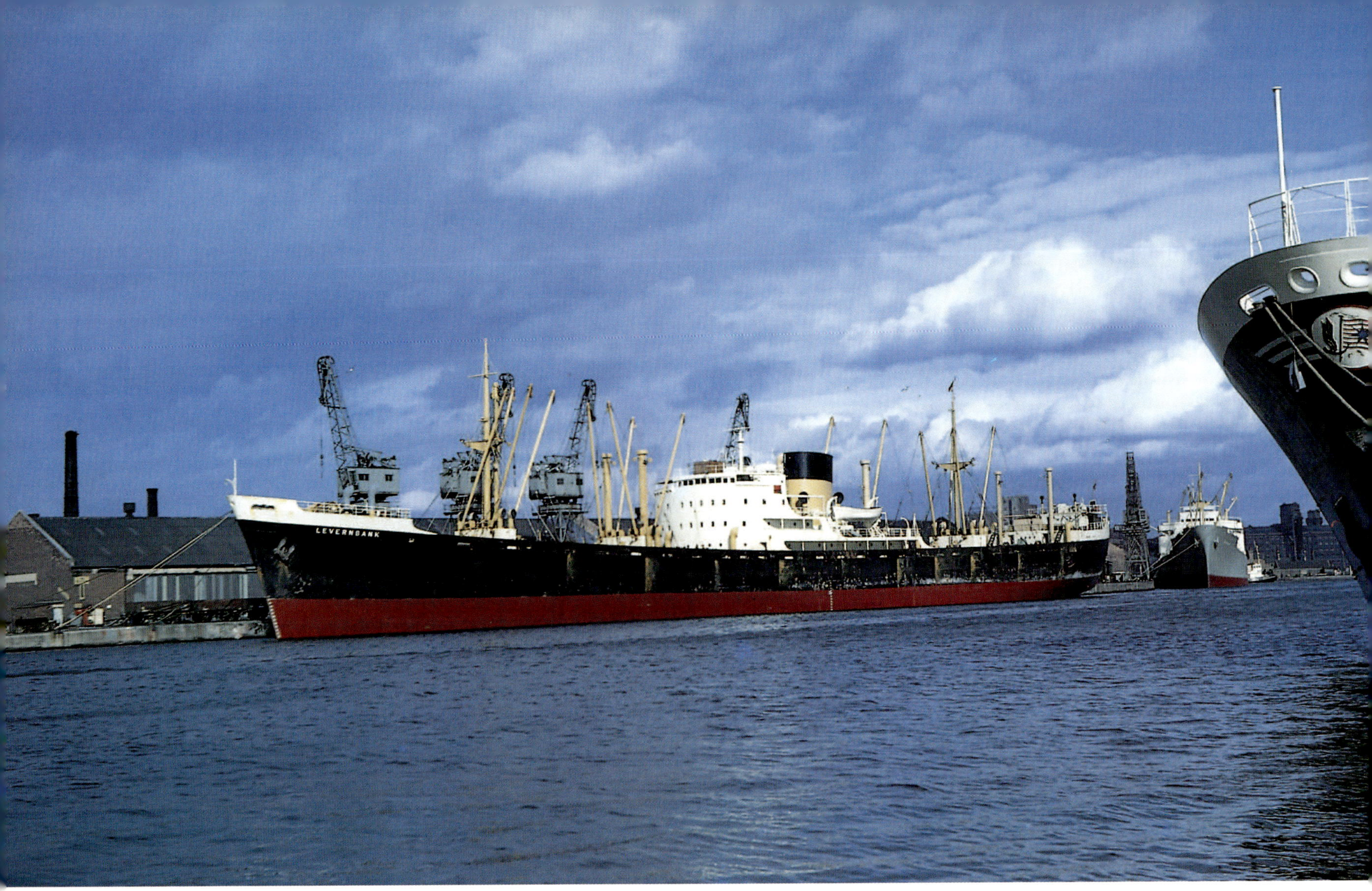

One of the foremost British operators of cargo ships was the Bank Line Ltd. Ships from its large fleet called at many UK ports and the Mersey was no exception. Here we see the ***Levernbank*** (8567grt/61) at Berth 223 in Birkenhead's West Float in the Spring of 1972. She was built at the Harland and Wolff shipyard in Belfast, and was one of seventeen vessels of a standard design known as HW2. Later vessels in the series had some detail differences, notably in the bridge/wheelhouse area. Launched on 28 April 1961, she was handed over to Bank Line on 11 August. She had heated tanks for the carriage of palm oil. She had a reasonably uneventful career until she ran aground on 9 July 1973 during a voyage from Chittagong to Buenaventura. She refloated two days later and was taken in tow but the tow parted and the ***Levernbank*** sank.

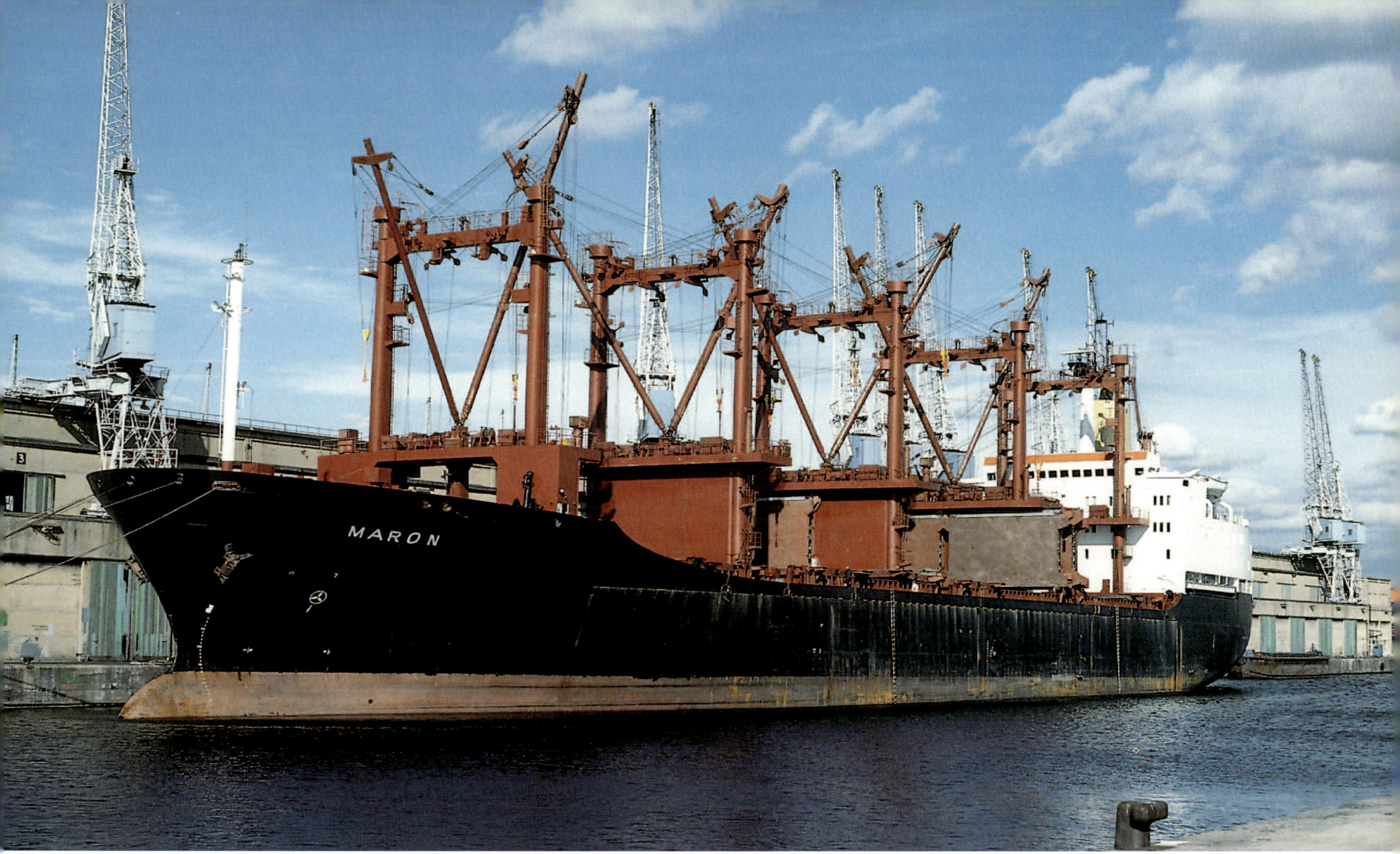

By contrast with the fine cargo liners which have graced the previous pages, we look at two vessels which were built to cope with the rapid growth of containerisation. We have already seen two examples of cargo ships thus built for operators in Africa on pages 36 and 37. Long-established British owners had to try to adapt. Blue Funnel, through its parent company of Ocean Transport & Trading, ordered a class of three ships from Scotts' Shipbuilding Co Ltd at Greenock. The first of these was the ***Maron*** (16482gt/80), seen at Berth 54 in Huskisson Branch Dock No. 1. Launched on 26 April 1979, she was handed over in April 1980. Renamed ***Studland Bay*** in 1982/83 while on charter to Overseas Containers Ltd, she was sold out of the fleet in 1986, the year after this photograph was taken, and the series of subsequent names often reflects her charterers. She became ***Baltic Adventurer***, ***Rainbow Avenue***, ***Merchant Patriot*** on three occasions, ***CMB Enterprise***, ***Woermann Ubangi*** and ***Lanka Amitha***. It was when named ***Merchant Patriot*** on 30 December 1997 that she suffered a flooded engine room and was abandoned off the Bahamas. She was towed to Freeport and later sold to Mexican breakers, arriving at Tuxpan on 25 June 1998.

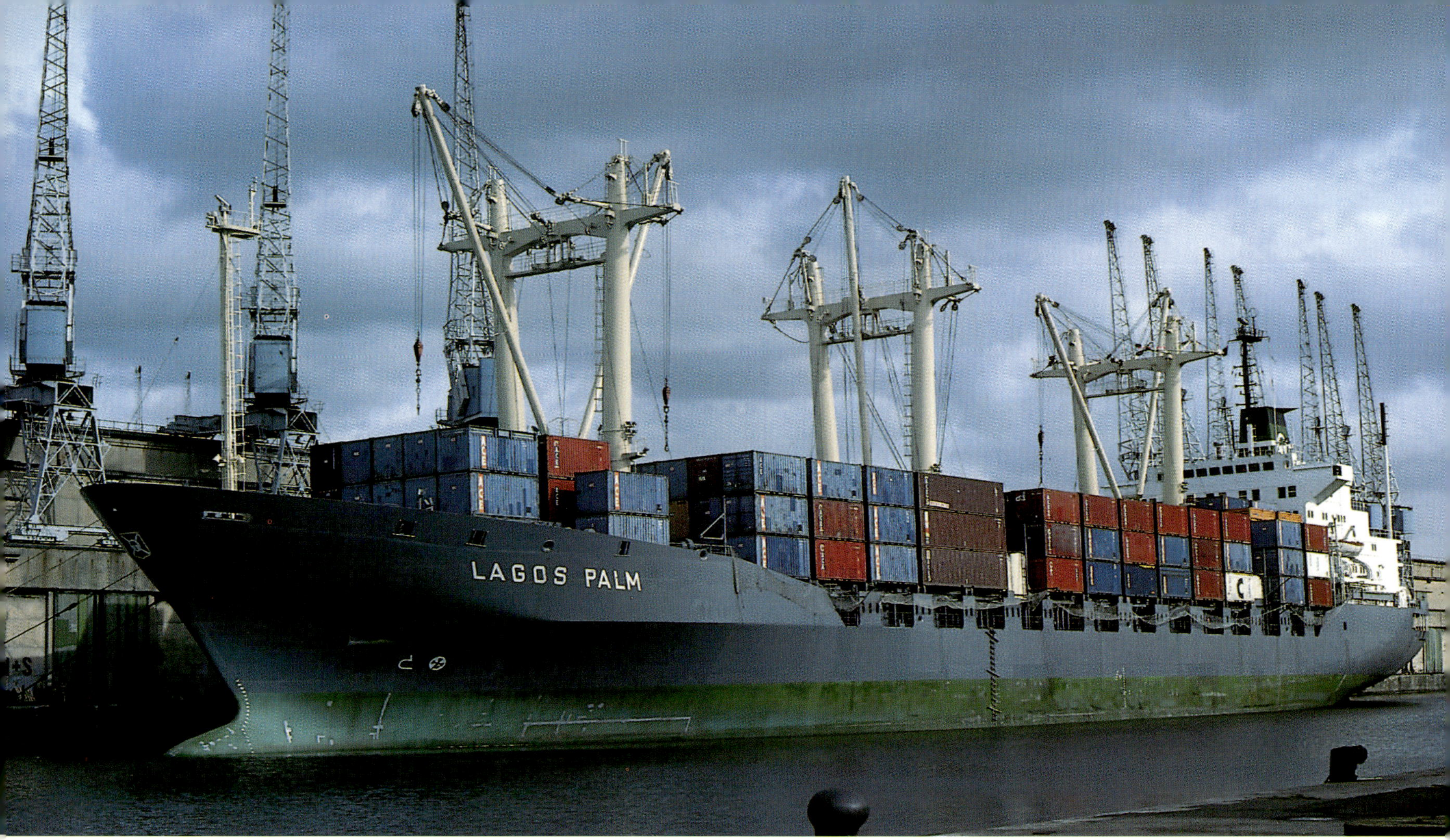

At the same berth is the ***Lagos Palm*** (15575grt/82). Palm Line was established in 1949 but had its origins over three decades earlier when Lord Lever sought to safeguard the supply of raw materials from West Africa for his soap and detergents business on Merseyside by forming and purchasing shipping companies which served the area. Palm Line was formed from an alliance between one of Lever's companies and the United Africa Company. Many would say that Palm Line's conventional cargo ships built in the 1950s were the finest of their type. By the early 1980s, sea transport had changed as we shall see on the next few pages. Palm Line ordered two new multi-purpose ships from the Stocznia Szczecinska shipyard in Poland. The ***Lagos Palm*** was the first of these and was an example of a standard design known as B181/II. She was launched on 21 August 1981 and completed on 31 July 1982. With chaos in West African ports in the early 1980s associated with difficult political and economic conditions, trade to that area was declining rapidly despite the appearance given in this view where she has a good load of containers. After only two years in service, the ***Lagos Palm*** was chartered in 1984 to Lloyd Brasileiro and renamed ***Lloyd Rio*** for service in South America. On completion of this charter, she returned to northern Europe and was briefly renamed ***Lagos*** prior to being sold in 1986 to Russian owners who gave her the name ***Boris Andreyev***. A decade later she was renamed ***Pearce*** and in 1998 she became ***Nieves B.*** under the Spanish flag, trading mainly from Spanish Mediterranean ports to the Canary Islands.

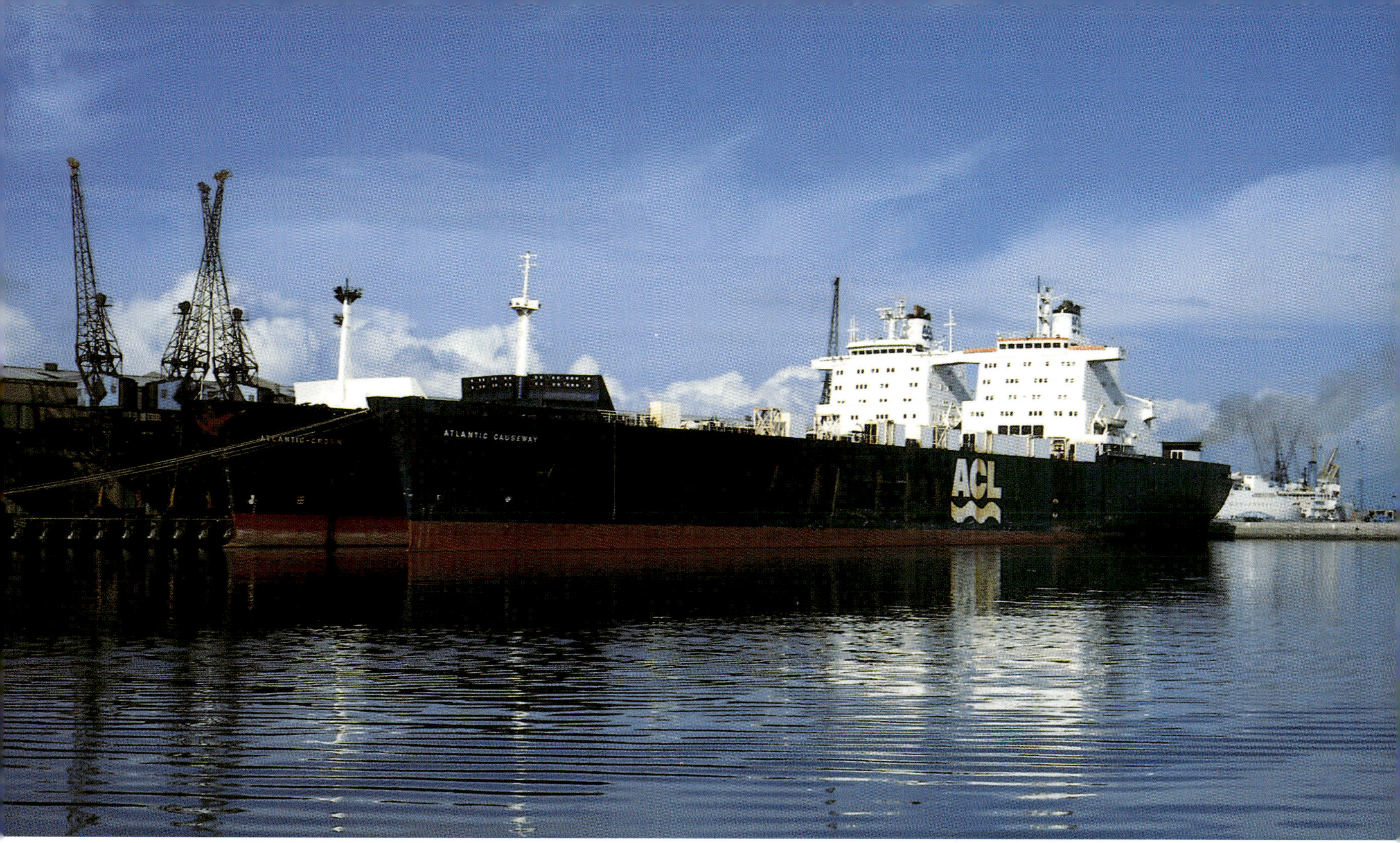

Atlantic Container Line (ACL) was an operating company founded in 1965 by Swedish ship owner Olaf Wallenius whose own Wallenius Lines was joined by the Transatlantic Steamship Co Ltd, Swedish America Lines, and Holland America Line. The purpose was to cope with the growing competition in transatlantic cargo services and also to raise the huge capital investment required for the containerisation of liner traffic on this route. Each of the four initial partners ordered a combined 700 TEU ro/ro container ship which was revolutionary in design at the time. The ships were owned by the individual companies and time-chartered to ACL. In 1966/67, the Cunard Steamship Co Ltd and Compagnie Générale Transatlantique joined the consortium. Cunard contributed two vessels to the consortium's second group of vessels. One was the ***Atlantic Conveyor***, lost so tragically in the Falklands campaign, and the other was the ***Atlantic Causeway*** (14946grt/69) which was built at the Swan Hunter shipyard at Walker on Tyneside. She was launched on 2 April 1969 and completed in November 1969. Her steam turbines were increasingly expensive to operate and she was laid up in Canada Dock, Liverpool, from 22 January 1983 to 22 April 1986 when she was sold to shipbreakers in Taiwan. This photograph was taken in Autumn 1984 during her period of lay-up. She was renamed ***Atlantic*** for the delivery voyage and arrived at Kaohsiung on 16 June 1986.

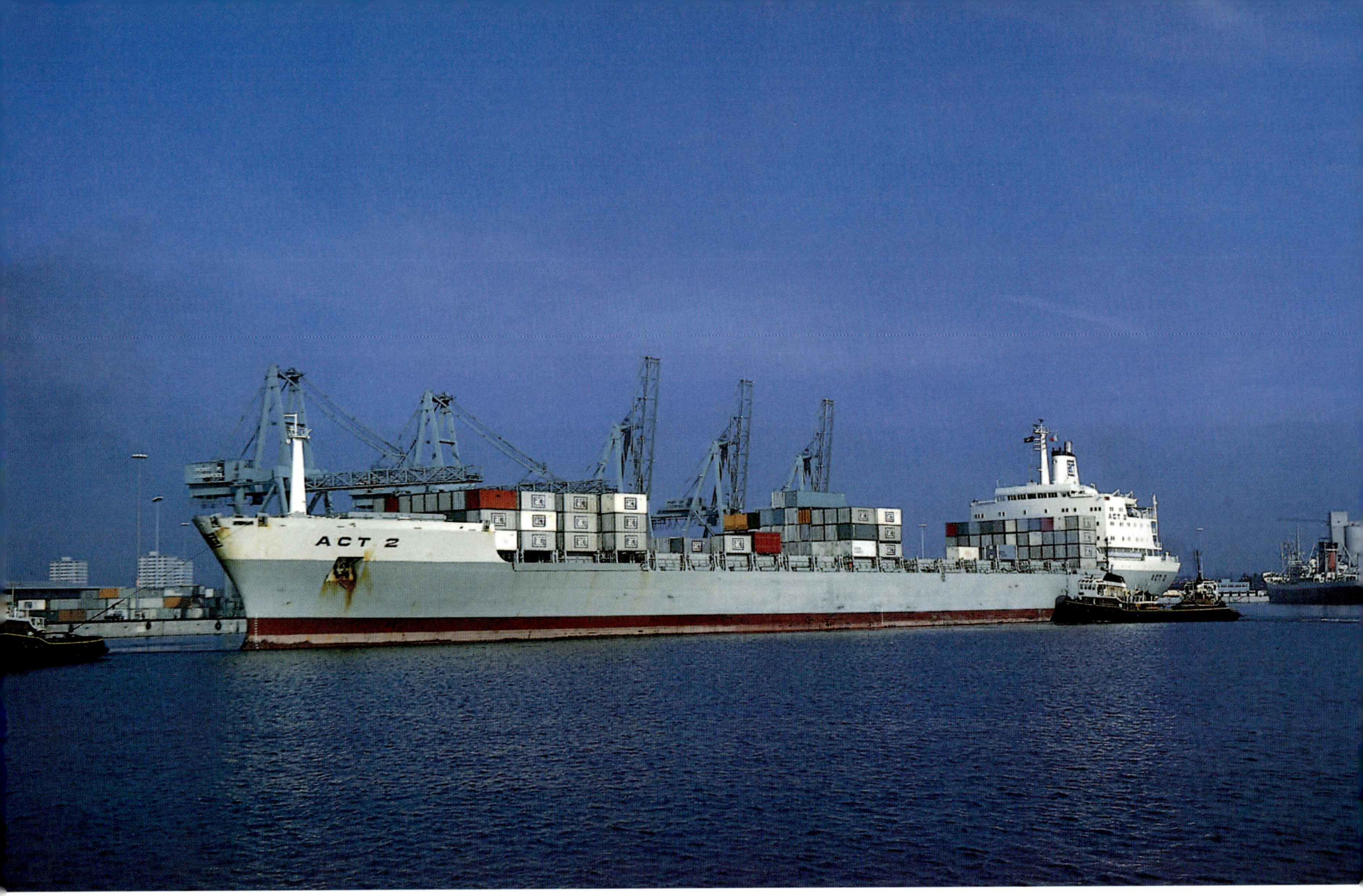

The ***ACT 2*** (24821grt/69) berthing at the Royal Seaforth Container Terminal in Autumn 1972. Associated Container Transportation Ltd (ACT) was a holding company set up jointly by a group of well-established British shipping companies. A subsidiary company, ACT(A) [Associated Container Transportation (Australia) Ltd], was established in August 1967 to handle the containerisation of the trade between the UK and Australia. Later in 1967, ACT(A) ordered three container vessels from the Bremer Vulkan shipyard in Vegesack, Bremen. The ***ACT 2*** was launched on 3 January 1969 and completed in May 1969. Between September 1983 and March 1984, she was renamed ***Los Angeles*** for the duration of a time charter to Johnston Scanstar Line. In 1991, she was sold to P&O Containers Ltd and was renamed ***Moreton Bay***. She arrived at Alang on 28 May 1998 to be broken up.

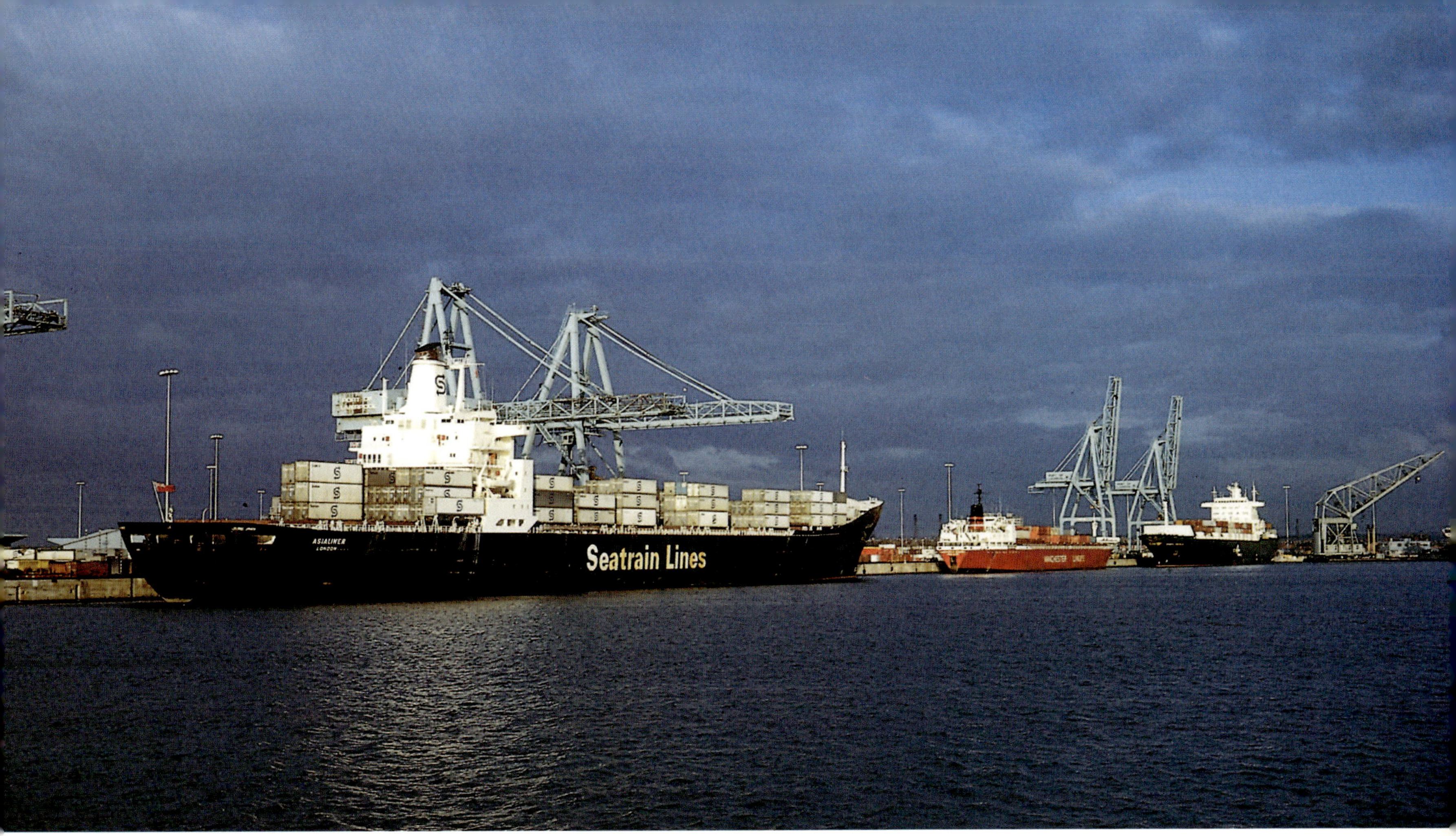

A general view of the container terminal in Royal Seaforth Dock on 11 October 1974. Nearest the camera is the ***Asialiner*** (30909grt/72) built at the Rheinstahl Nordseewerke shipyard in Emden and launched on 21 September 1971. Unusually powered by two gas turbine engines, she operated a transatlantic service. Her subsequent names display the frequent change of charterers for she later became ***Seapac Bunker Hill*** (1981), ***Oriental Minister*** (1981), ***Dart Europa*** (1987), ***OOCL Europe*** (1988), ***Ville de Titana*** (1996), ***Med Colombo*** (1997) and finally ***Chicago Express*** (1997). She was demolished at Alang in 2001. Astern of her is the ***Manchester Courage*** (12039grt/69), built at Smiths Dock on the River Tees and launched on 23 September 1968. By the time of this photograph, the Manchester Liners service to Canada had been transferred to Liverpool from Manchester. She became ***Pacific Container*** in 1979 and ***MSC Marina*** in 1989. Having arrived at Antwerp as ***MSC Marina*** on 26 February 1992, she left on 4 April for her delivery voyage to breakers at Alang, arriving there on 28 April 1992. *Lloyd's Register* suggests that she bore the name ***Hangkwai*** in 1989; this may have been during a stay in the port in June but she seems not to have traded as such. There is no problem with the name of the third vessel, ***Atlantic Cinderella*** (DEU, 15347grt/70). Launched as such on 29 August 1969 at the Dunkerque yard of Ateliers & Chantiers de Dunkerque & Bordeaux, she kept that name until demolished at Kaohsiung where she arrived on 19 January 1986.

(C J Tabarin)

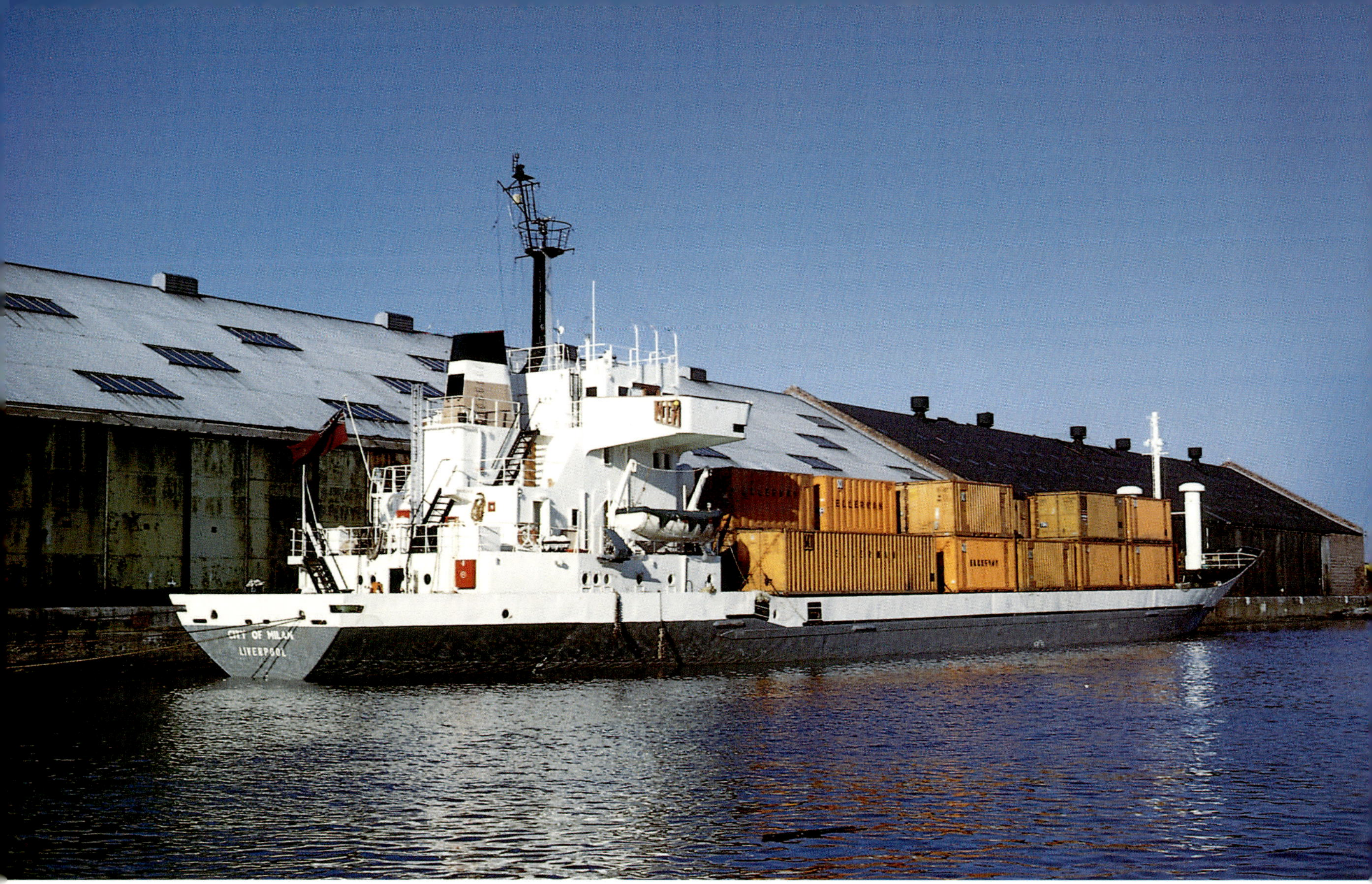

The ***City of Milan*** (1578gt/69) was the first of a group of nine container ships known as the Hustler class. Eight of these were built for James Sherwood's Sea Containers Limited against a long-term time bareboat charter to Ellerman Lines for service from the Mersey to the Mediterranean. Built by A Vuijk & Zonen at Capelle a/d IJssel, she was completed as ***Minho*** in December 1969. In 1974, she was renamed ***City of Milan***, thus conforming to the conventional Ellerman naming scheme. Under this name, she is seen waiting in West Hornby Dock, Liverpool, on 12 October 1974. In 1979, she was sold and renamed ***Eco Mondego***, being noted as laid up with surveys overdue in late 1984. She became ***Ana Raquel*** in 1989 but *Lloyd's Register* lists no owner for her during most of the 1990s. She was sold for demolition at Lisbon in late 2001.

(C J Tabarin)

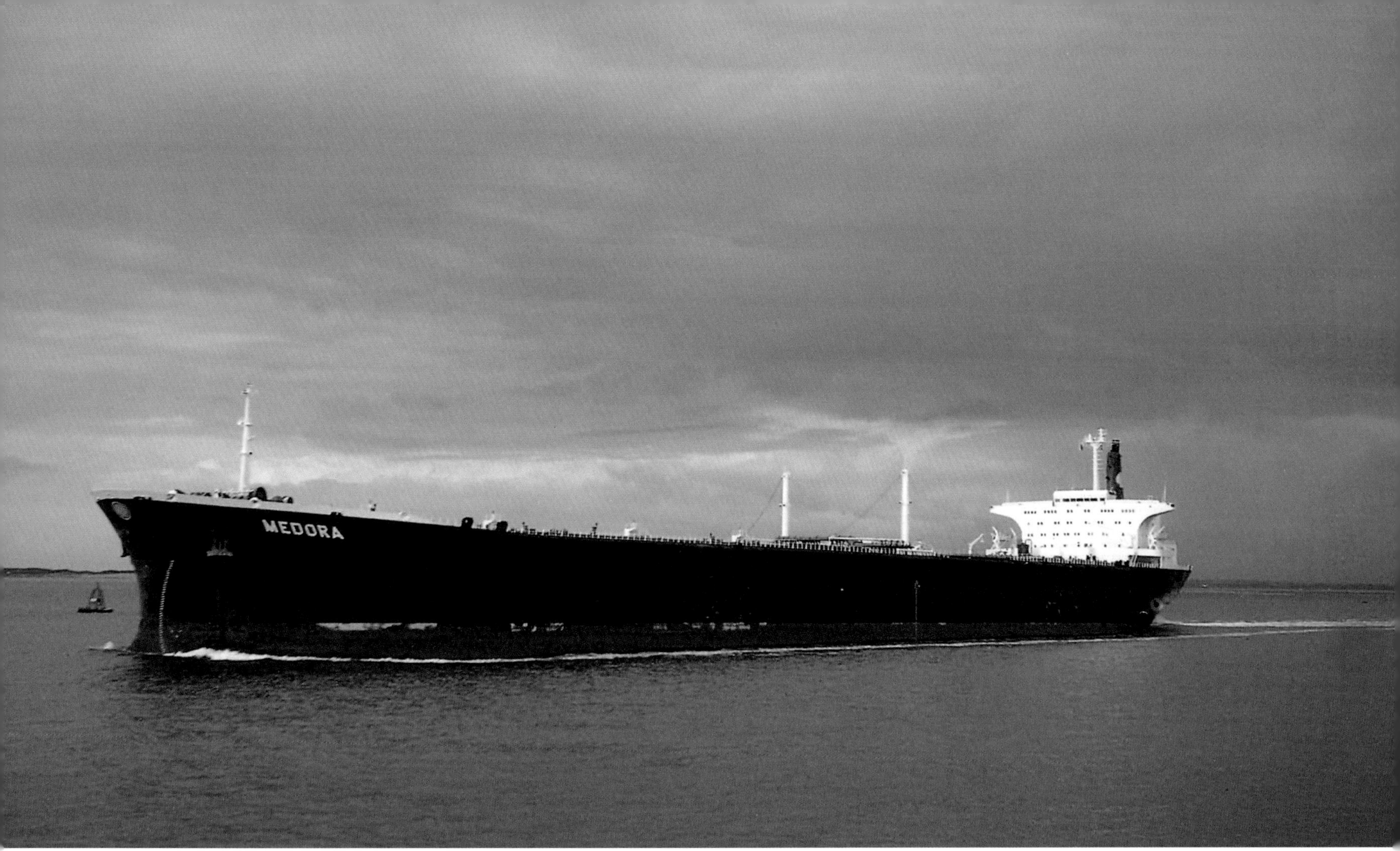

As the size of crude oil tankers grew during the 1960s, it was evident that a new deepwater terminal would have to be built to handle the tankers bringing crude oil for the Shell refinery at Stanlow on the Manchester Ship Canal. This terminal and associated tank farm was at Tranmere on the Wirral side of the Mersey. In the late 1960s and 1970s, Shell's M-class tankers were frequent callers bringing crude oil from the Middle East. Seen here in July 1972 is the ***Medora*** (105252grt/68), built by Mitsubishi Heavy Industries in Nagasaki. Like many steam turbine tankers of her generation, she had a short working life and was sold in 1979. She was then converted at the La Ciotat shipyard in Marseilles into a production vessel for the Fulmar oil field in the North Sea where she was based from 1981 until replaced by a new vessel in 1994. During her period in this role, she broke her moorings on Christmas Eve 1988 and was towed to Stavanger four days later. She was towed to Rotterdam for permanent repairs in March 1989 and returned to service six months later. Laid up at Stavanger for three years from 1994, she left in March 1997 when she was towed to Singapore by the ***Smit London***. There she was converted yet again, becoming the floating production facility ***Jabiru Venture*** to operate in the Timor Sea off north-west Australia where she is used to pump high pressure gas.

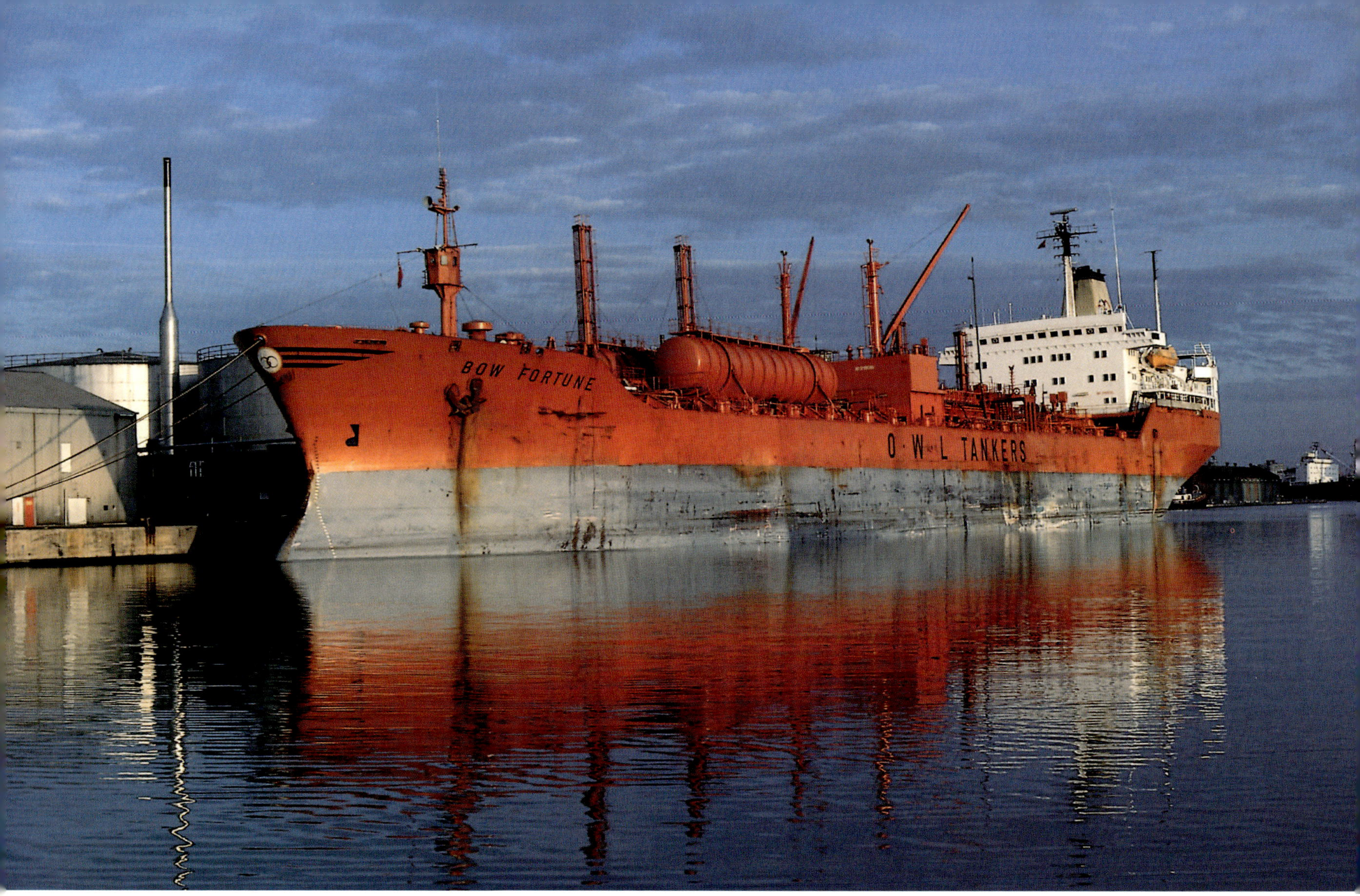

Over the last decade, a huge amount of redevelopment has taken place within the Birkenhead dock system and it is certain that this process will continue, and that shipping will ultimately be displaced from the area. In addition to general cargo and huge quantities of grain, the docks in Birkenhead have traditionally handled cargoes of molasses, edible oils and chemicals though these commodities have been brought by smaller tankers in recent years. An example of the larger tankers to have called is the ***Bow Spring*** (NIS, 17561gt/76), one of a pair of tankers built in the mid-1970s by Stocznia Szczecinska im A Warskiego in Szczecin. She was renamed ***Bow Neptun*** in 2004 and remains in service as such in mid-2007.

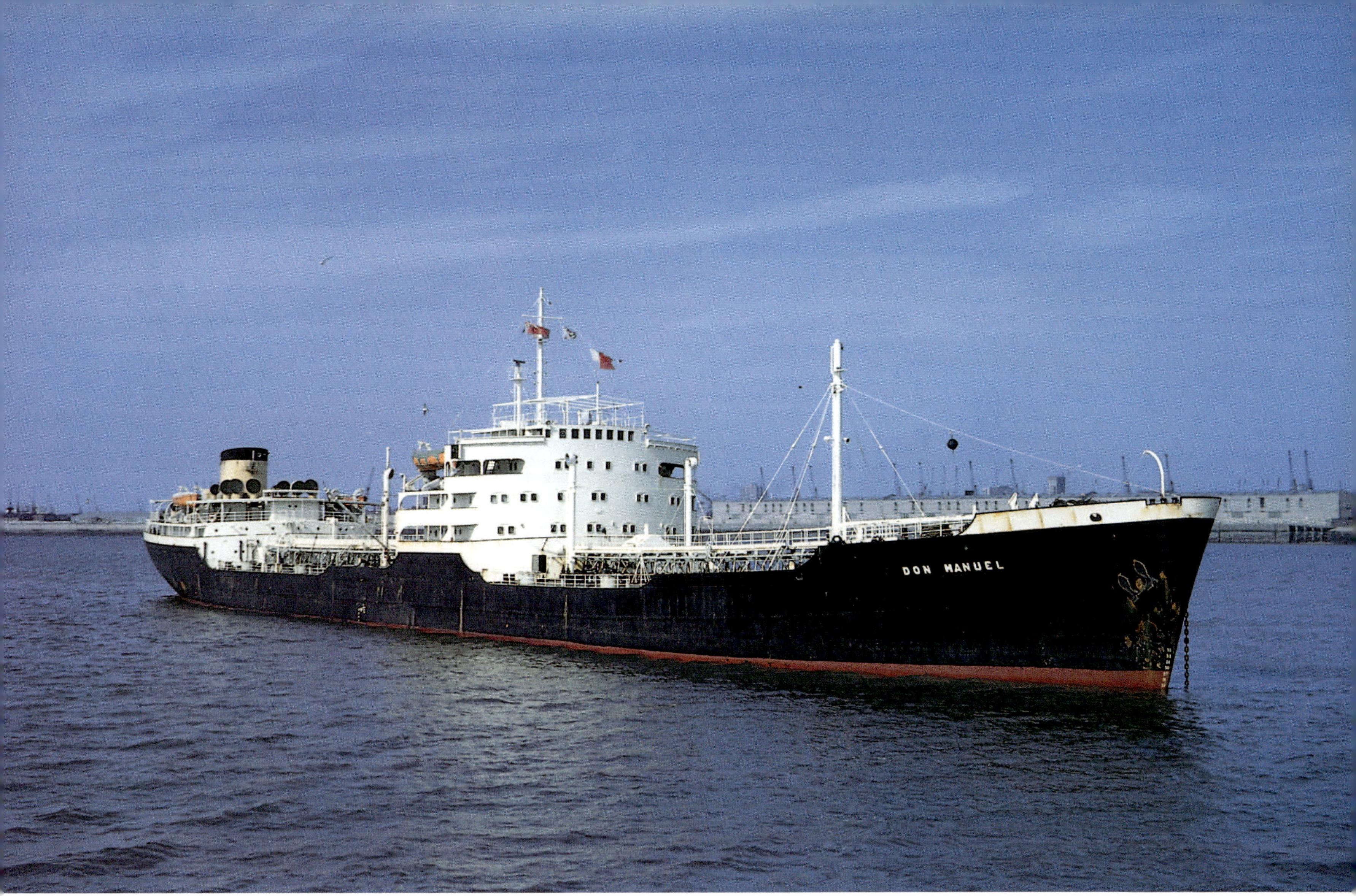

The ***Don Manuel*** (ESP, 11675grt/52) is seen at anchor in the Mersey in Spring 1970. She was probably awaiting high water before sailing up to Eastham and the Manchester Ship Canal. Her attractive bridge-amidships profile is typical of the multi-purpose tankers built in the 1950s. She began life as ***London Victory***, built for London & Overseas Freighters by the Furness Shipbuilding Co Ltd at its Haverton Hill yard on the River Tees. She was sold to Spanish owners in January 1965 and renamed ***Don Manuel***. Ultimately sold to Spanish shipbreakers, she arrived at Bilbao for demolition on 18 March 1974, with work commencing some two months later.

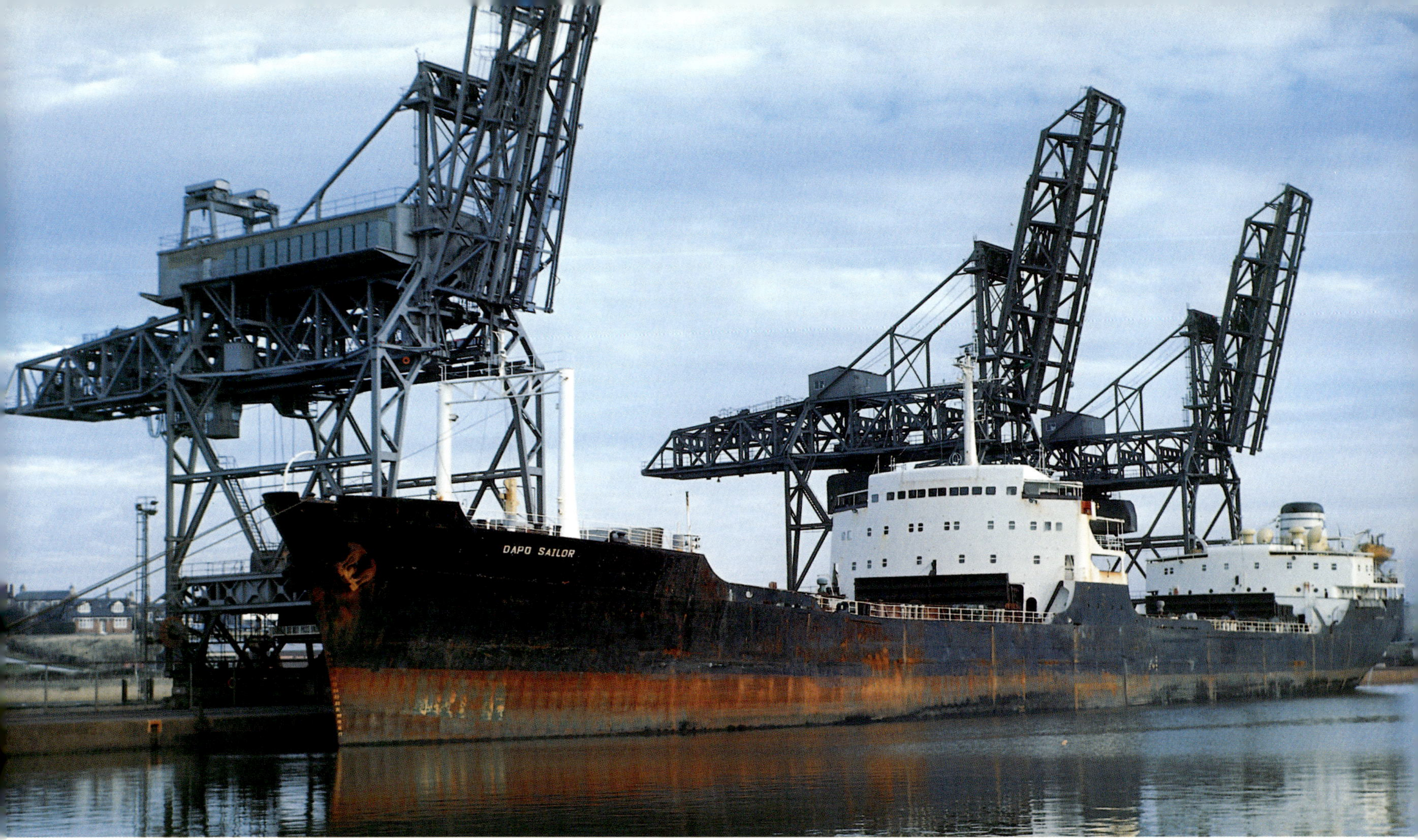

Raw materials for the John Summers steel works at Shotton on the River Dee, some 20 miles (32 km) south of the Mersey, were delivered to Bidston Dock in Birkenhead. A total of 73 purpose-built ore carriers were constructed between 1952 and 1963 for charter to the British Iron & Steel Corporation, generally known as BISCO. Four were built by the Blyth Dry Dock and Shipbuilding Co Ltd for St Denis Shipping Co Ltd, in which BISCO had a 49% share and Wm Cory and Sons Ltd a 51% share. The second vessel in the group was the ***Monksgarth***, launched on 1 December 1959 and handed over in April of the following year. On completion of their time charters, the ore carriers were sold and the Greek Pothitos group bought several of them, some being renamed with "Dapo" prefixes which derived from the first two letters of the surnames of two partners, Davaris and Pothitos. Thus the ***Monksgarth*** became ***Dapo Sailor*** when acquired in 1977. Short term charters to what had by then become British Steel continued. Transfer within the Greek company saw her become ***Evpo Sailor*** in autumn 1978, the new prefix coming from the name Evangelos Pothitos. She was sold for demolition five years later, arriving at Alang near Karachi on 27 November 1983. The ***Dapo Sailor*** (GRC, 10760grt/60) discharges iron ore at Bidston Dock on 26 November 1977.

(Bernard McCall)

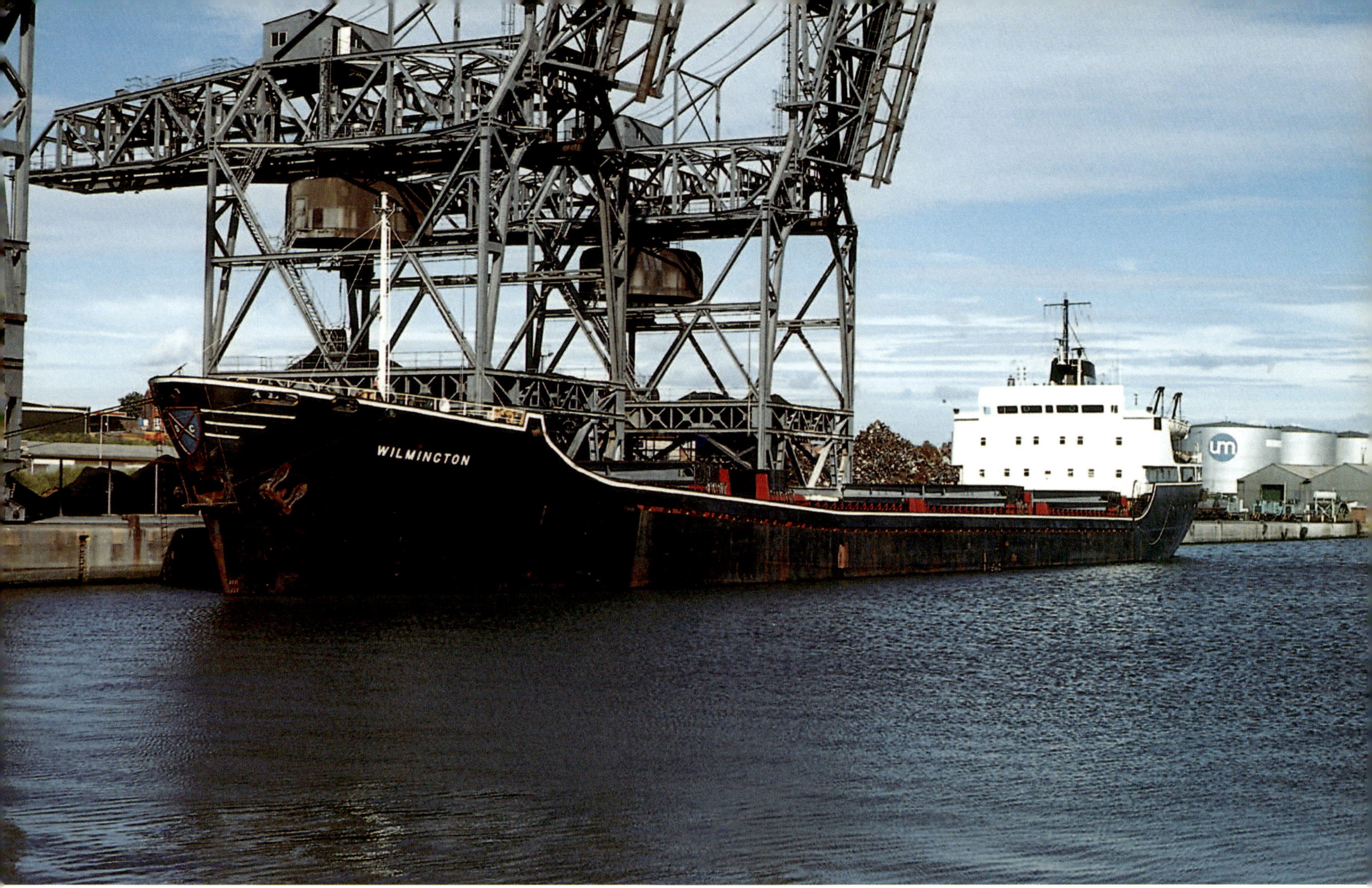

Photographed in Bidston Dock in 1985 is Stephenson Clarke's ***Wilmington*** (5689grt/69). By this date, the dock was no longer used for ore imports and it is doubtful if the ***Wilmington*** would have loaded scrap, piles of which can be seen on the quayside. She had brought a cargo of coal which would be taken by rail to Fiddlers Ferry power station. She was built at the Hall, Russell shipyard in Aberdeen and completed in September 1969. She had a relatively short life and was sold for demolition at Zeebrugge where she arrived on 17 May 1986. Bidston Dock was opened in 1933 but the gantry unloaders were not built until 1952 when the north side of the dock began to be used for imports of iron ore for the then-new steel works at Shotton. Steel manufacture at this works ceased in 1980 and the cranes were used mainly to discharge coal. They were eventually demolished in 1992.

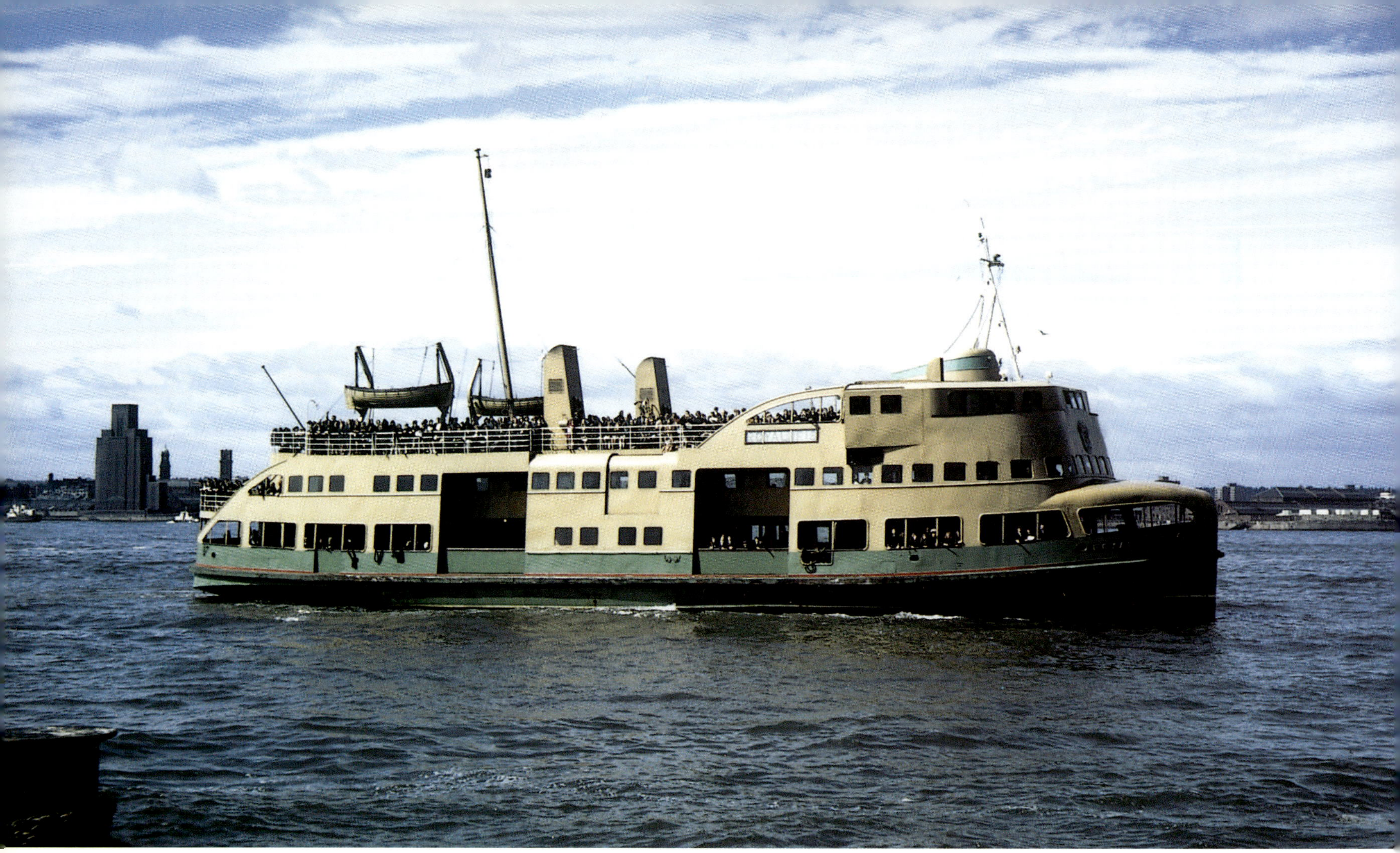

We now move on to look at some passenger-carrying vessels. Taking advantage of post-war optimism, Wallasey Corporation placed an order for three ferries to be delivered in the early 1950s. The first was the twin-screw diesel- electric ***Royal Iris*** (1234grt/51), intended as a dual-purpose ferry and river cruise vessel. Built at the Denny shipyard in Dumbarton, she was launched on 8 December 1950. Her streamlined superstructure and rounded bow gave her a futuristic appearance and she was known as "The Electric Iron" on Merseyside. Here we see her off the Pier Head at Liverpool. The green livery and buff upperworks, replaced with a blue/white livery in 1970, did not enhance her appearance but she is remembered with great affection, another of her nicknames being the "fish and chip boat". Taken out of service in 1991, she was sold ostensibly for use as a restaurant ship in 1993 and was moved to Cardiff in 1995 and to London in 1999. It is a matter for regret that she has become so neglected over the last decade. It is unfortunate that she cannot be returned to the Mersey for the Capital of Culture celebrations in 2008. Many locals consider her to be iconic as she played such an important part in the social life of the city and many of the famous pop groups of the 1960s performed on her cruises.

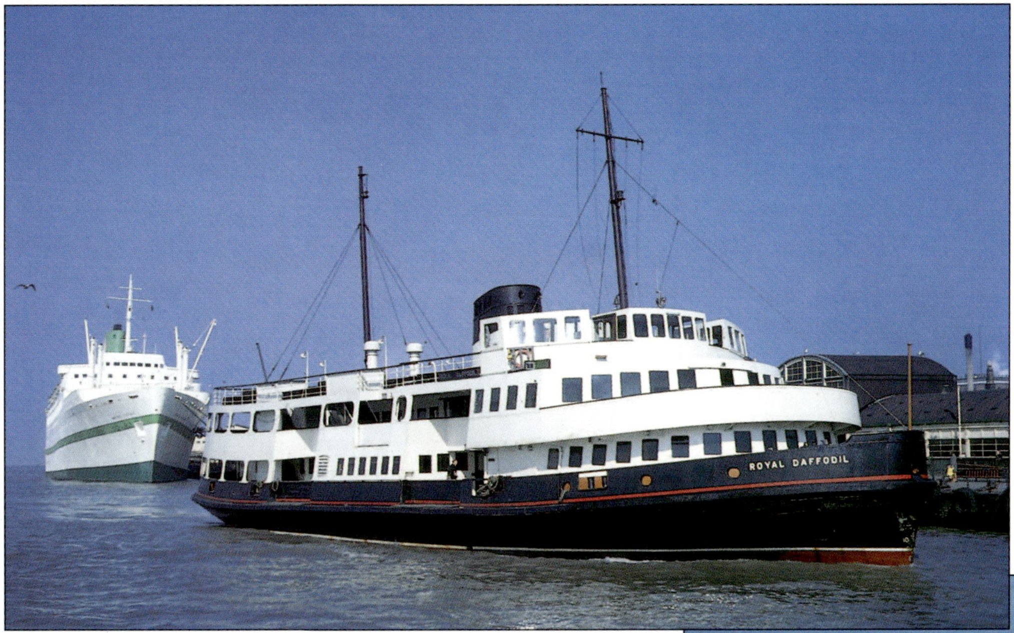

In the late 1950s, the ***Royal Daffodil II*** (609grt/58) joined the fleet of Mersey ferries. Although ownership is generally credited to Wallasey Corporation, the registered owners were in fact "The Mayor, Aldermen & Burgesses of the County Borough of Wallasey" - a delightfully historic title. She was built at the James Lamont & Co Ltd shipyard in Port Glasgow and was launched on 6 December 1957, with delivery coming in April 1958. The suffix "II" was necessary because the General Steam Navigation Co Ltd already had an excursion ship named ***Royal Daffodil***. When this vessel was taken out of service in 1966, the Mersey ferry became ***Royal Daffodil*** in 1968 after the demolition of the GSN vessel. She had a relatively short career, being considered in the mid-1970s as too small for cruising but too large for the ferry service. She was sold to Greek buyers in April 1977 and was converted to a vehicle ferry. She was renamed ***Ioulis Keas II***, becoming ***Agia Kyriaki*** in 1990.

The ***Mountwood*** (464grt/60) exemplifies the present generation of Mersey ferries but as this is a volume of "memories", we see her in the livery applied to the ferries for the first UK International Garden Festival held in Liverpool in 1984. A product of the Philip & Sons shipyard in Dartmouth, she was built for Birkenhead Corporation unlike the ***Royal Iris*** and ***Royal Daffodil***. She achieved fame in the 1960s when she was used as the setting for the song "Ferry 'cross the Mersey" and also appeared in the sitcom "The Liver Birds". In 2001/2, she was re-engined and refurbished. She re-entered service in April 2002 under the name ***Royal Iris of the Mersey***.

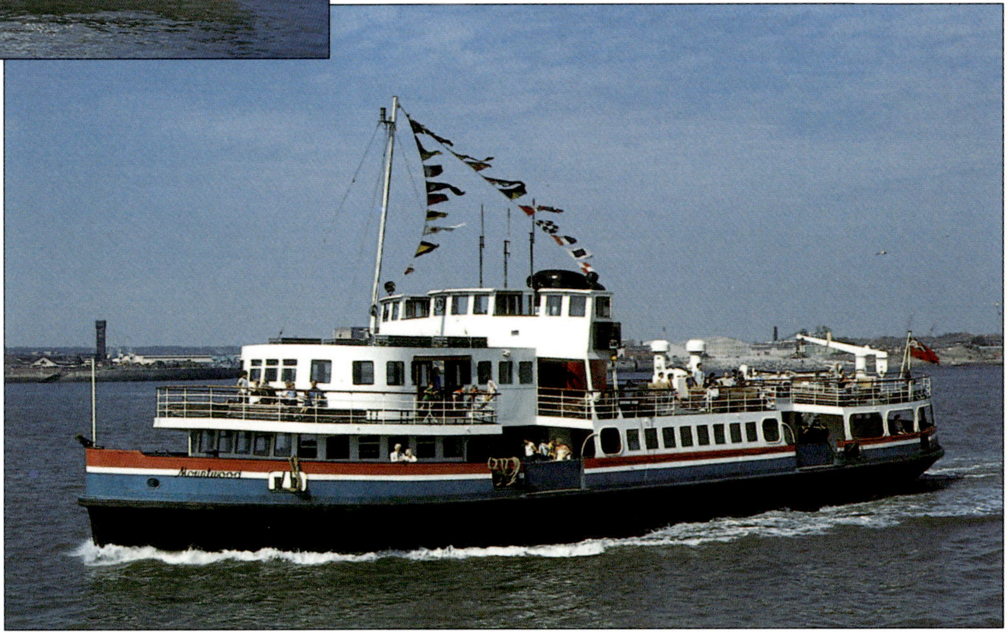

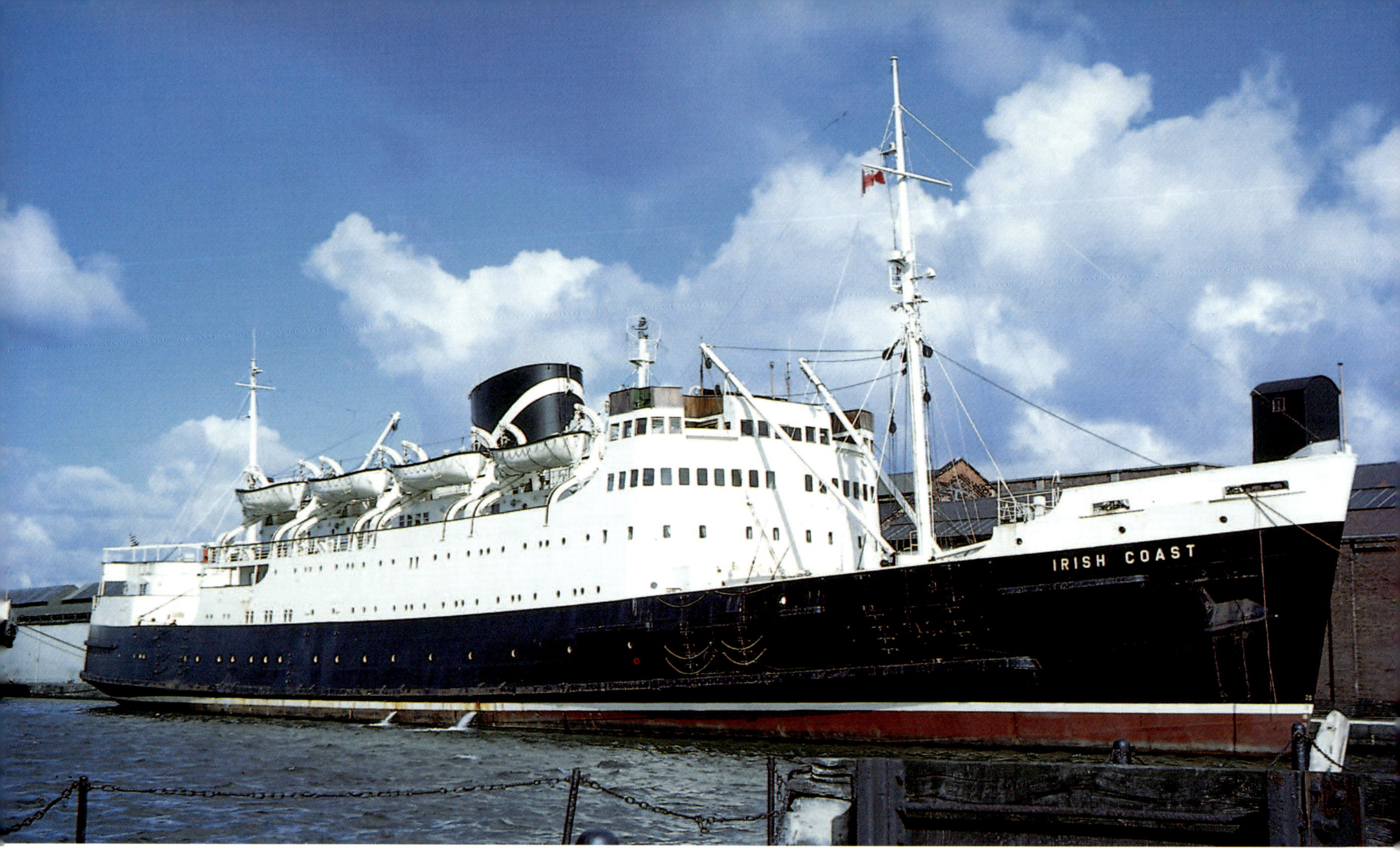

The name The Coast Line appeared in April 1917 when it was used in advertisements of Powell, Bacon and Hough Lines, a consortium of three coastal shipping companies formed four years previously. Over the years, the Coast Lines group acquired more and more smaller shipping companies, many of whose vessels kept the funnel colours of their original owners. The ***Irish Coast*** (3813grt/52) was the only large diesel ferry to keep the black funnel with white chevron throughout her career. She was launched at the Harland & Wolff shipyard in Belfast on 8 May 1952 by the wife of the Chairman of Coast Lines. Costing £800,000, she was designed for summer and autumn service on the Glasgow - Dublin route with relief work on other Irish Sea services during the winter. She was a luxuriously appointed ferry. In August 1957, she took up the summer-only day service between Ardrossan and Belfast. By 1968, she was surplus to requirements and here we see her in Morpeth Dock, Birkenhead, where she arrived for lay-up on 11 April 1968. Sold to the Epirotiki company later in the year, she was renamed ***Orpheus*** and then in 1969 was renamed ***Semiramis I***, ***Achilleus*** and ***Apollon II*** in quick succession, finally becoming ***Regency*** in 1981 following sale to the Philippines. She was wrecked during a hurricane at Batangas in October 1989 and broken up at Manila.

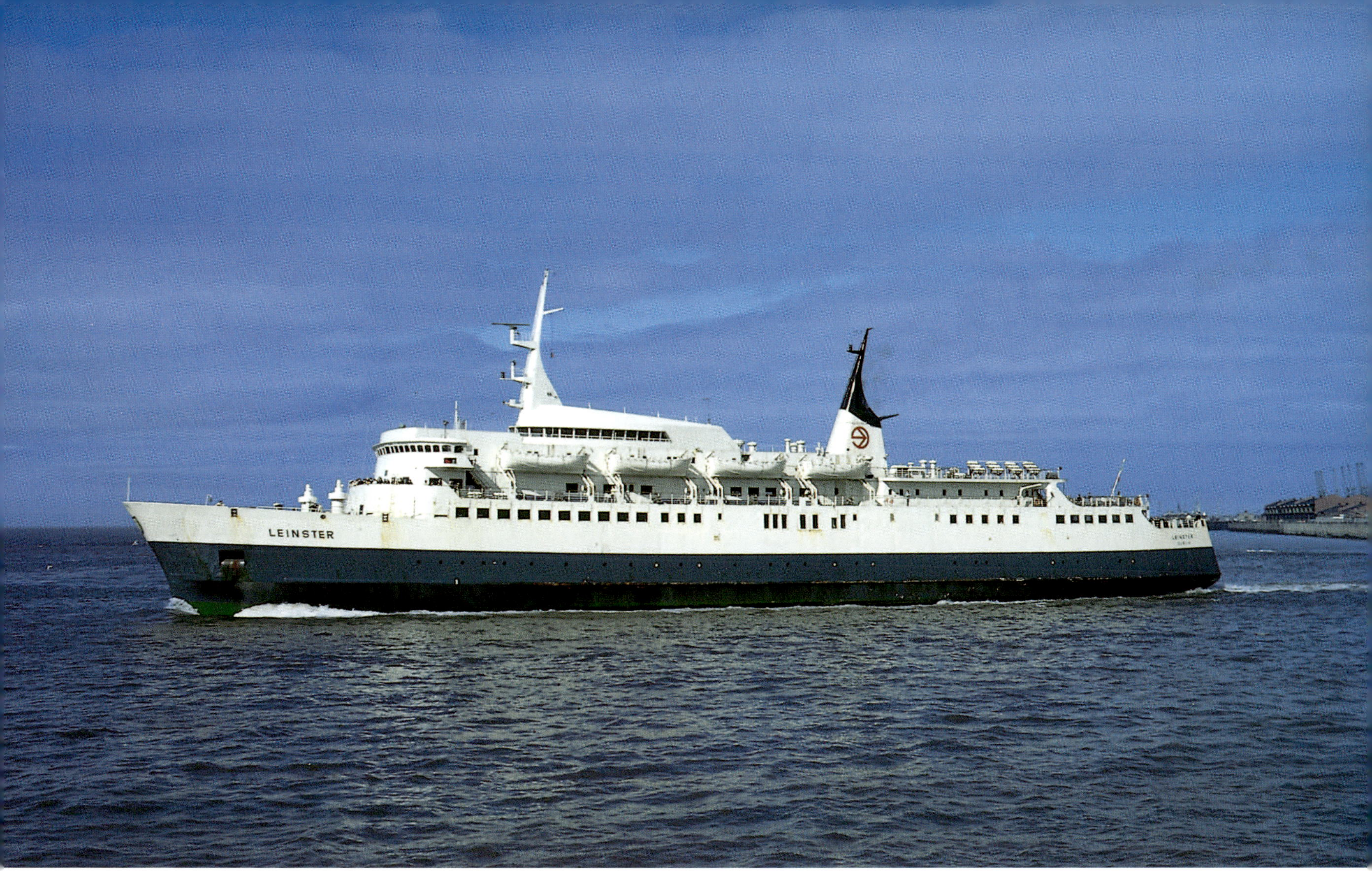

The ***Leinster*** (IRE, 4849grt/69) is an example of the first generation of ro/ro ferries on the Irish Sea which replaced the classic ferries such as the previous ***Leinster*** seen on the front cover. She was built by Verolme Cork Dockyard Ltd at Cobh and was launched on 19 November 1968. She was handed over to the British & Irish Steam Packet Company (B&I) in May 1969. She is seen here in April 1971. Renamed ***Innisfallen*** in 1980, she continued to serve the Irish Sea routes until sold to Mediterranean buyers in 1986 when she became ***Ionian Sun***. In 1990, she was chartered for the Swansea - Cork service and seems to have carried the unofficial name ***Celtic Pride II*** at least on a bridge board for part of this time. In 1993, she was renamed ***Chams*** for the duration of a charter to a Tunisian company and then reverted to ***Ionian Sun***. A new career beckoned in 2001 when she was sold to owners in the United Arab Emirates and she traded in the Middle East as the Dubai-registered ***Merdif***. She was sold for demolition in 2004.

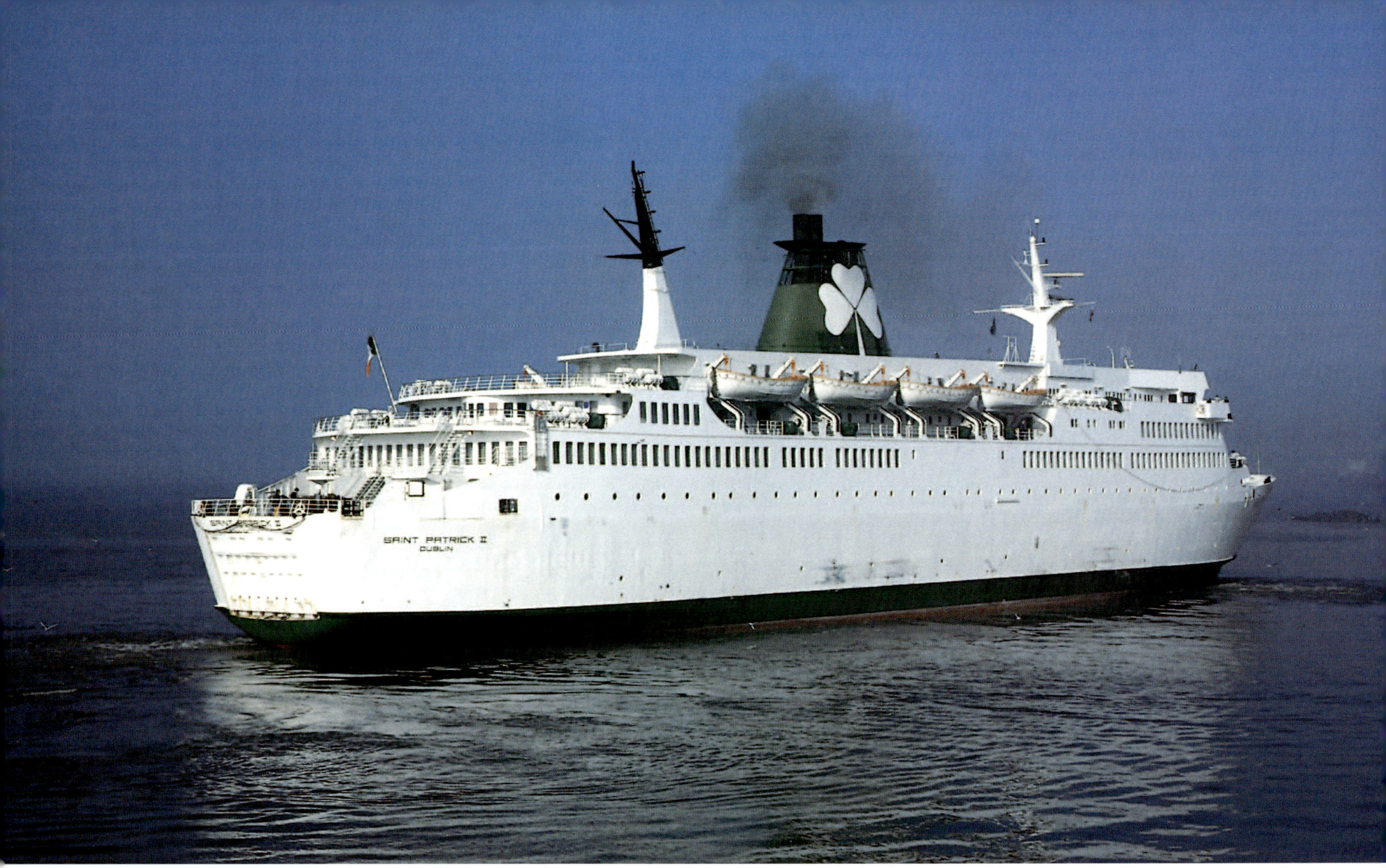

The J J Sietas shipyard at Neuenfelde on the outskirts of Hamburg is well-known for the construction of cargo vessels but in the early 1970s, it won the contract to build a ferry for SF Line, better known as Viking Line, for service between Sweden and Finland. Named ***Aurella*** and of 7210grt, she was launched on 17 March 1973 and handed over on 23 June. She left the Baltic in 1982 when purchased by Irish Continental Line for its Irish Sea service. Renamed ***Saint Patrick II***, she served until 1982 although she did have periods on charter to other routes. She was sold for service in the Mediterranean in 1998, becoming ***Egnatia II*** and was renamed ***Ville de Sete*** for a short charter in 2000 prior to being renamed ***City of Cork*** for service on the Swansea - Cork route. In 2002, there was another change in her area of operation when she was bought by Canadian owners and renamed ***C. T. M. A. Vacancier***. Under this name she operates a weekly round trip from Montreal to the Madeleine Islands with calls at Quebec and Chandler.

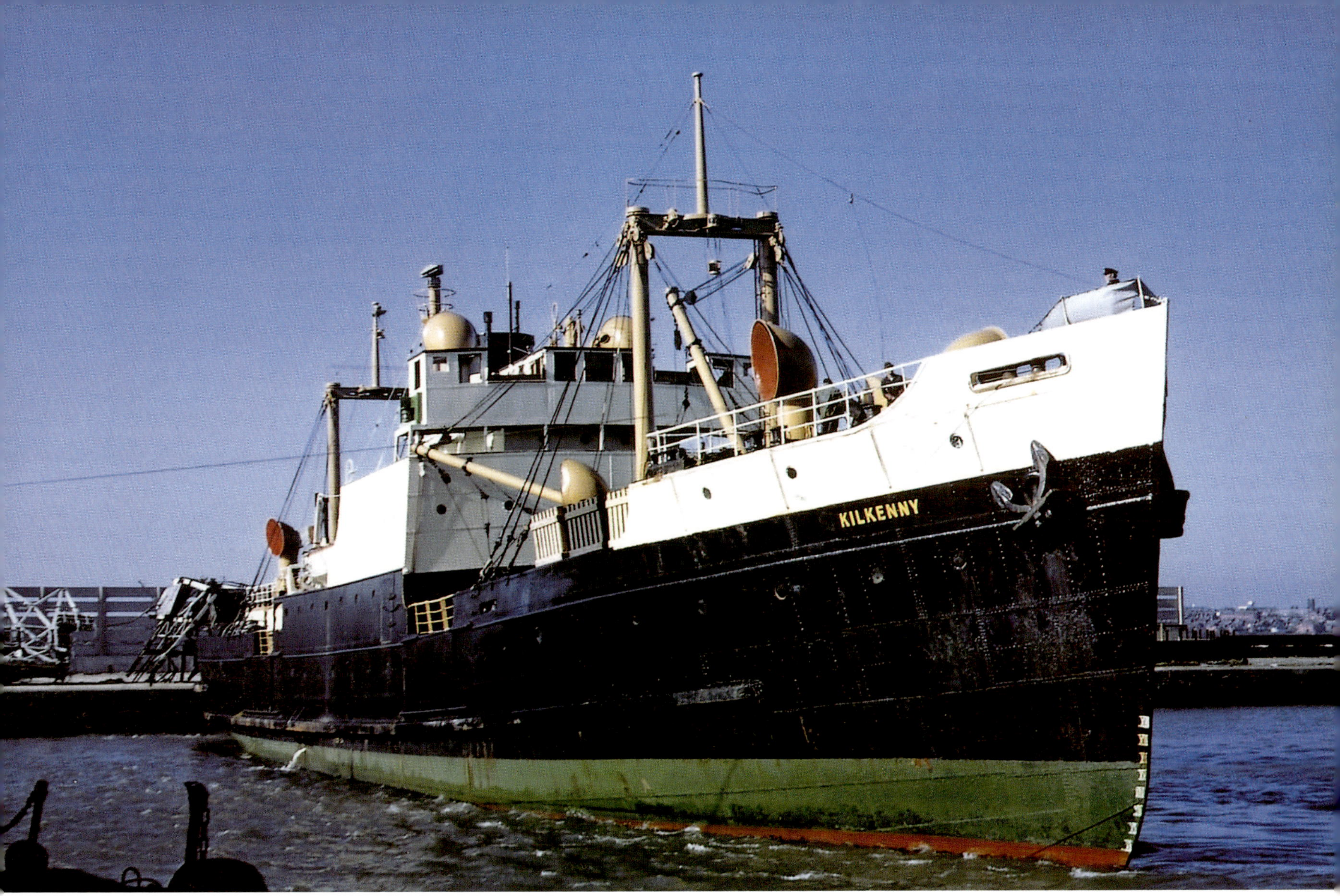

The cargo and cattle vessel ***Kilkenny*** (IRE, 1320grt/37), owned by the British & Irish Steam Packet Company, turns in Waterloo Dock as she arrives from Dublin and prepares to berth in Princes Dock. She was built by Dublin Dockyard Co, Vickers (Ireland) Ltd, and was powered by a 2-stroke 6-cylinder engine manufactured by Harland & Wolff. She was launched on 14 April 1937, completion being in July 1937. She was renamed ***Cork*** in 1971. On 27 May 1974, she suffered engine failure when off Holyhead and was initially towed to Dublin. Deemed unworthy of repair, she was sold for breaking up in Dalmuir in 1974.

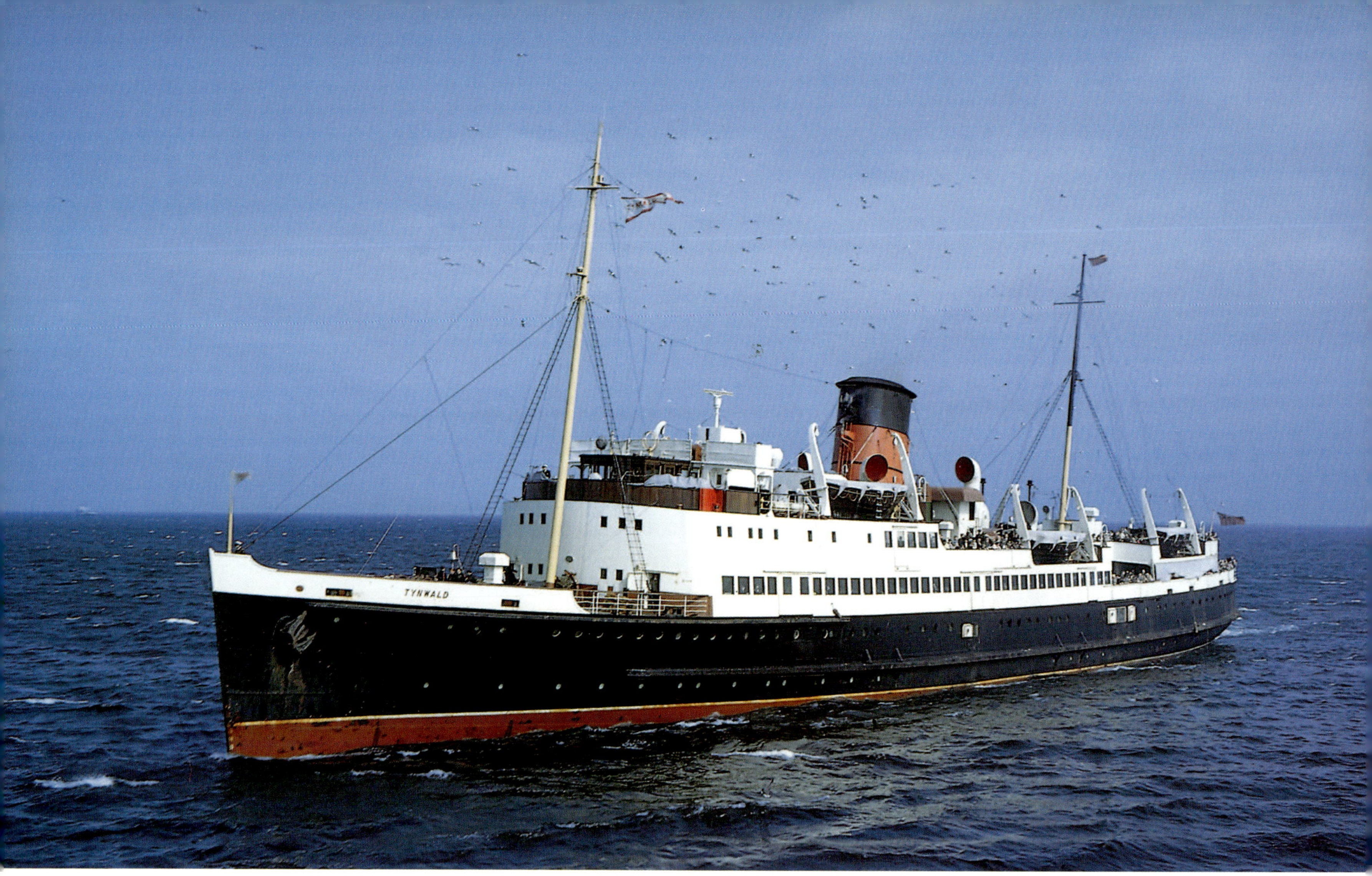

Generations of Merseysiders will have fond memories of the elegant passenger ferries of the Isle of Man Steam Packet Co Ltd. Even if they did not sail on them (and many did), they would see them at the Pier Head landing stage on a daily basis. There will be especially fond memories of the last generation of classic passenger vessels which served the island before the introduction of multi-purpose ro/ro ferries as seen on the next page. Attended by seagulls on a late summer day in 1968, the ***Tynwald*** (2487grt/47) was the fifth Steam Packet vessel to bear this name. She was built by Cammell Laird & Co Ltd at Birkenhead and was launched on 24 March 1947. The third of six basically similar vessels from her builder, she entered service on 31 July 1947. It was on 26 August 1974 that she made her final crossing and was then sold for demolition at Newport, Gwent. However, she was later resold for demolition in Spain and was towed to breakers at Aviles in February 1975.

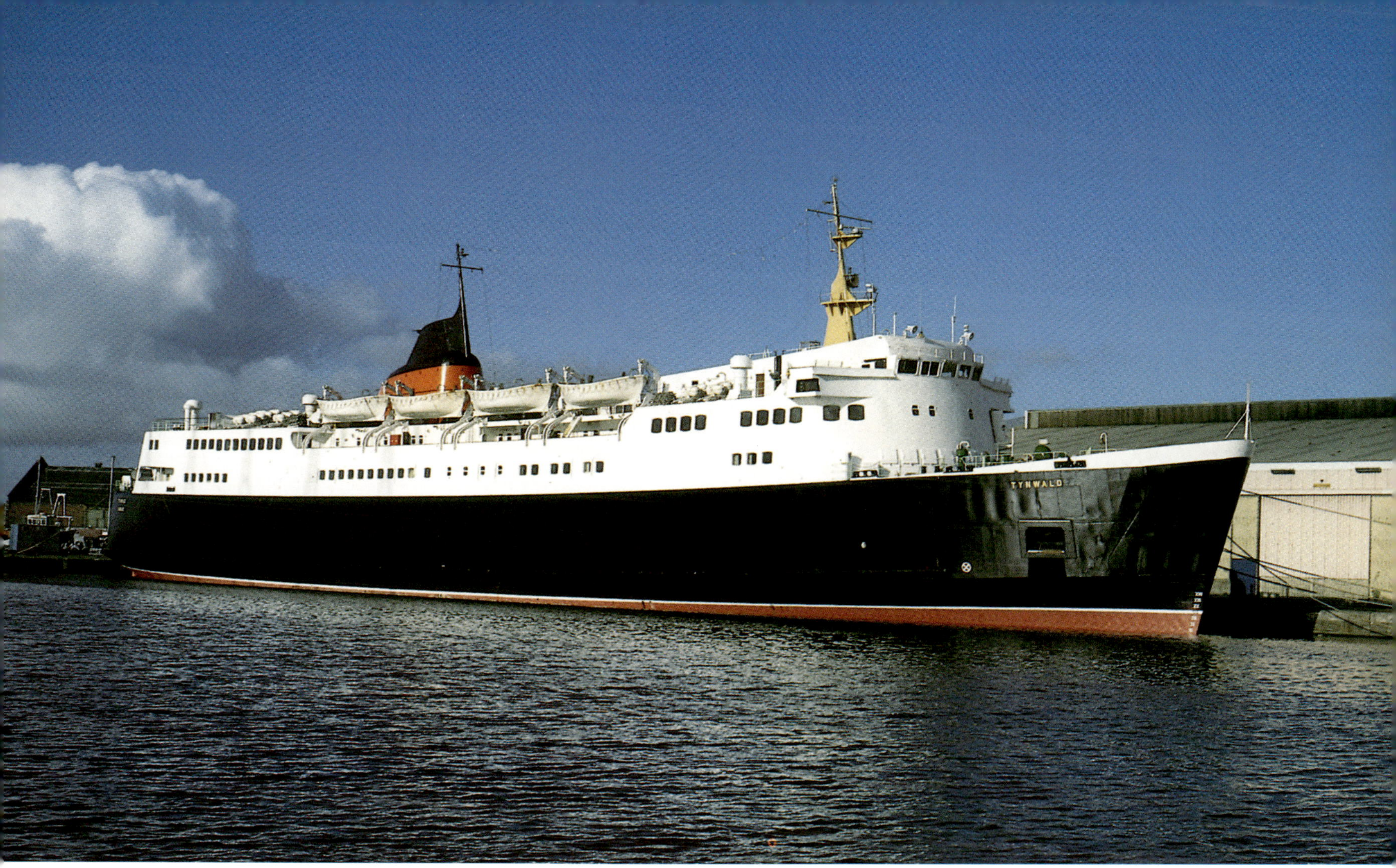

Appropriately we now look at the next ***Tynwald***. The mid-1980s were troubled times for the Isle of Man Steam Packet Co Ltd; indeed some would say that the troubles have continued since then. Be that as it may, tourist numbers were declining rapidly and the financial problems of the company in 1984/85 were acute. Consequently a merger was proposed with the rival Manx Line. Services to the island would henceforth be based on Heysham as the mainland port. The ***Tynwald*** (IOM, 3762gt/67) was chartered for the Heysham route. She was built as ***Antrim Princess*** for Caledonian Steam Packet (Irish Services) Ltd. A product of the Hawthorn Leslie shipyard at Hebburn, she was launched on 24 April 1967. Eventually coming into British Rail ownership, she had the distinction of being that company's first diesel-powered drive-through ferry. Her charter to the Steam Packet company began on 5 October 1985 and she entered service the next day. She made her final voyage on 19 February 1990 and was then laid up in the River Fal before being sold to Italian owners and renamed ***Lauro Express***. Sold on in 2003, she was renamed ***Giuseppe D'Abundo*** and then became ***Stella*** in 2006. She arrived at Alang for demolition on 19 January 2007.

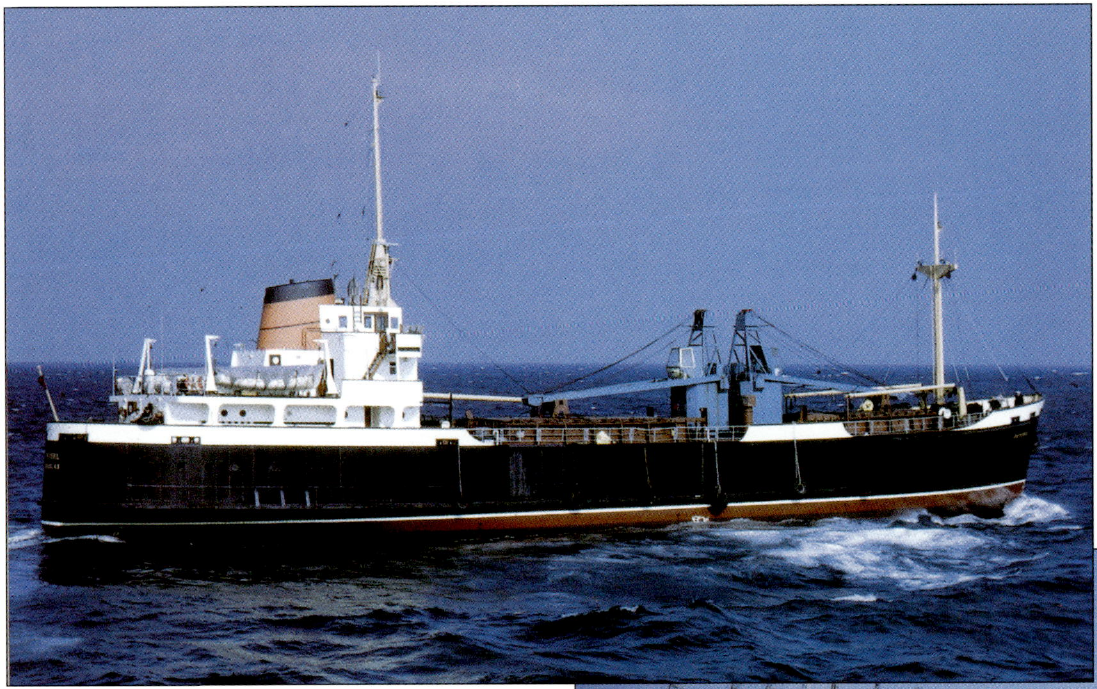

The ***Peveril*** (1534grt/64) was built for the Isle of Man Steam Packet Co Ltd by the Ailsa Shipbuilding Co Ltd at Troon and cost £279, 921. Sources differ about the date of her launch, some quoting 3 December 1963 and others saying 6 December. She arrived at Douglas from her builders on 7 March 1964 and entered service the next day. In 1972, she was converted to a cellular container vessel with a 56 TEU capacity, incredibly modest by today's standards. This conversion increased her gross tonnage from her original 1048grt. We see her here in both guises. In the view on the left, she has her original cargo handling gear.

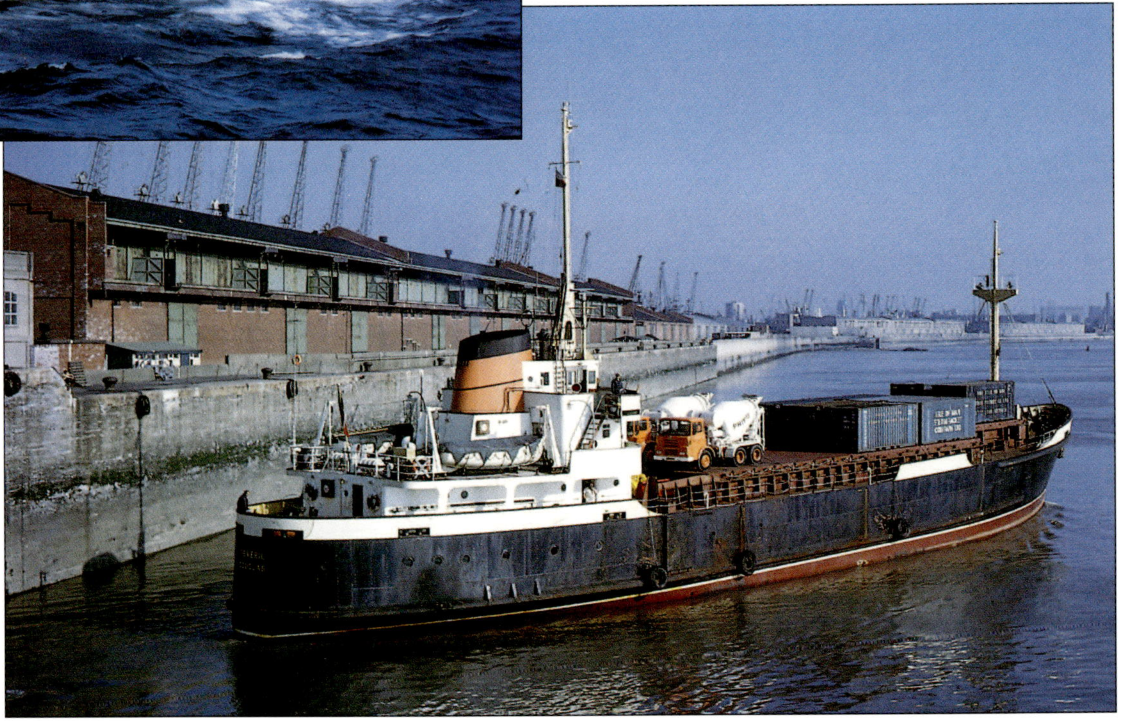

She was photographed as she entered the Mersey from Gladstone lock on 6 May 1975. Rather surprisingly, *Lloyd's Register* continued to claim that she had cargo handling gear even as late as 1979/80. She made her final voyage for the Isle of Man company on 19 June 1981 and was sold for further trading, becoming ***Nadalena H***. The next decade witnessed a series of name changes as she became ***Virginia Luck*** (1982), ***Akak Princess*** (1983), ***Zeina*** (1984), ***Akak Star*** (1986), ***Mariana I*** (1991) and ***M.J.K. V*** (1992), ***Ayah*** (1999) and ***Mihmandar*** (2000). She arrived at Aliaga under tow on 12 April 2001 to be broken up.

(C J Tabarin)

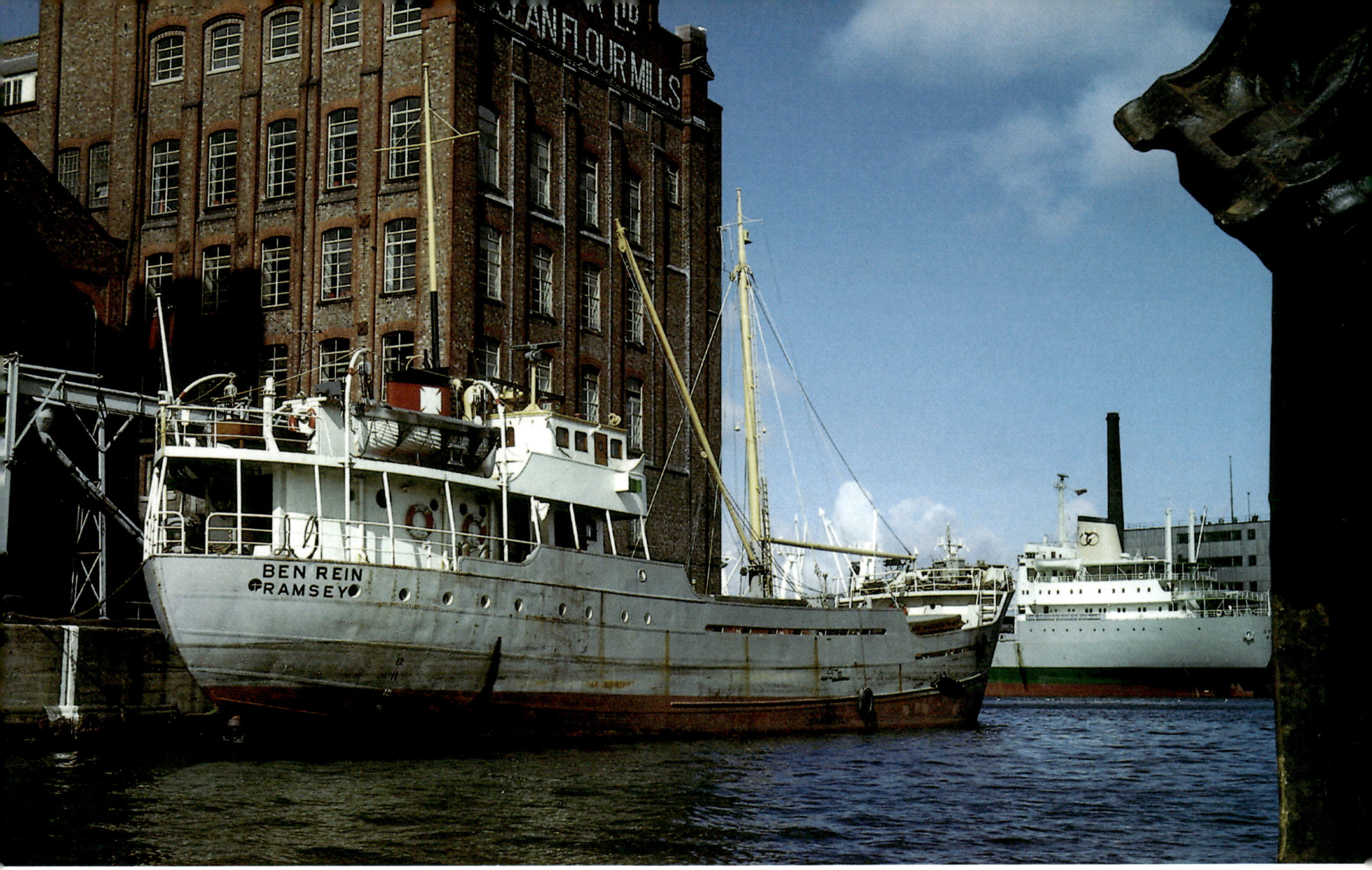

Coasters of the Ramsey Steamship Company Limited have long had an important role to play in supplying the Isle of Man from the UK mainland, especially from Liverpool and other ports on the Mersey. The ***Ben Rein*** (IOM, 393grt/47) was built as ***Lita*** and launched on 31 July 1947. Although a classic Dutch-built coaster, a product of Scheepswerf Delfzijl v/h Sander, she was handed over to her original Norwegian owners in November 1947. She was sold within Norway and renamed ***Tamara*** in 1954. She was acquired by the Ramsey company in July 1956 and renamed ***Ben Rein***, a name meaning "Queen" in the Manx language. She had the distinction of being the first motor vessel in the Ramsey fleet. After sixteen years service, she was sold to Greek owners by whom she was renamed ***Gianna P***, becoming ***Kaponas Th*** in 1975 and ***Agia Moni*** in 1979. She reverted to ***Gianna P*** in 1980. Her ultimate fate is uncertain; she remained listed in *Lloyd's Register* in 2003 but was deleted after this date.

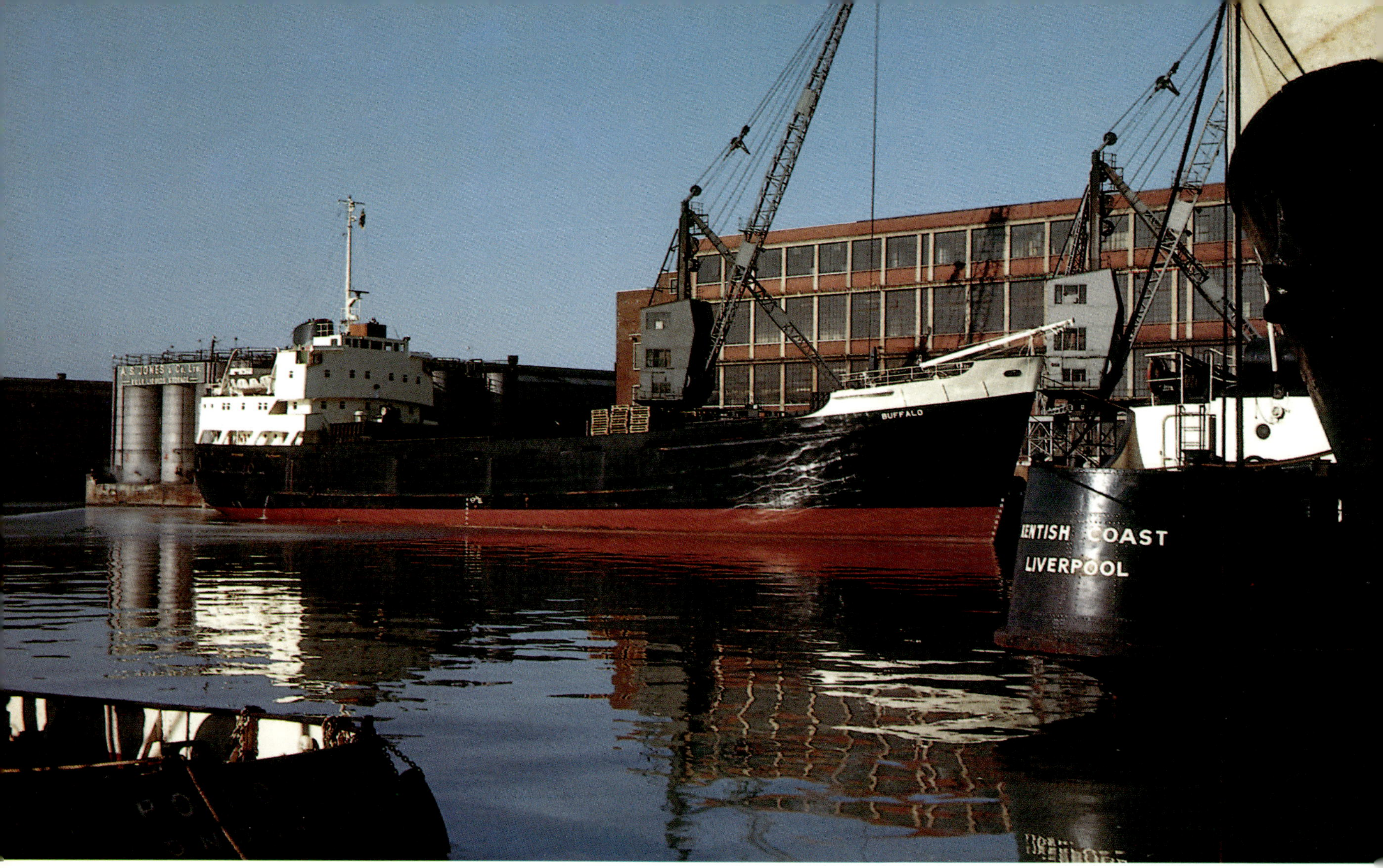

Not all vessels in the Coast Lines fleets had "Coast" names. The ***Buffalo*** (2163grt/62) was built by Ardrossan Dockyard Ltd. She was launched on 2 May 1961 but not delivered until January 1962. After a decade as a conventional cargo ship, she was converted to a fully cellular container carrier with a 101 TEU capacity and was renamed ***Norbrae*** in 1972 and the ***Roe Deer*** in 1974. In 1977, she was sold out of British ownership and she crossed the Atlantic to trade on the east coast of Canada and the USA as ***Newfoundland Container***. Laid up and with surveys overdue in January 1984, she eventually found buyers in the Caribbean and in 1985 was renamed ***Caribbean Victory***, becoming ***Lefkimmi*** in 1986 and the ***St George*** in 1988. Four years later she was renamed ***Container Express***. Her subsequent history is unclear. *Lloyd's Register* still lists her under this name but some sources suggest that she has been renamed ***Triana Cayman***. If she continues to trade, her survival is noteworthy irrespective of her present name.

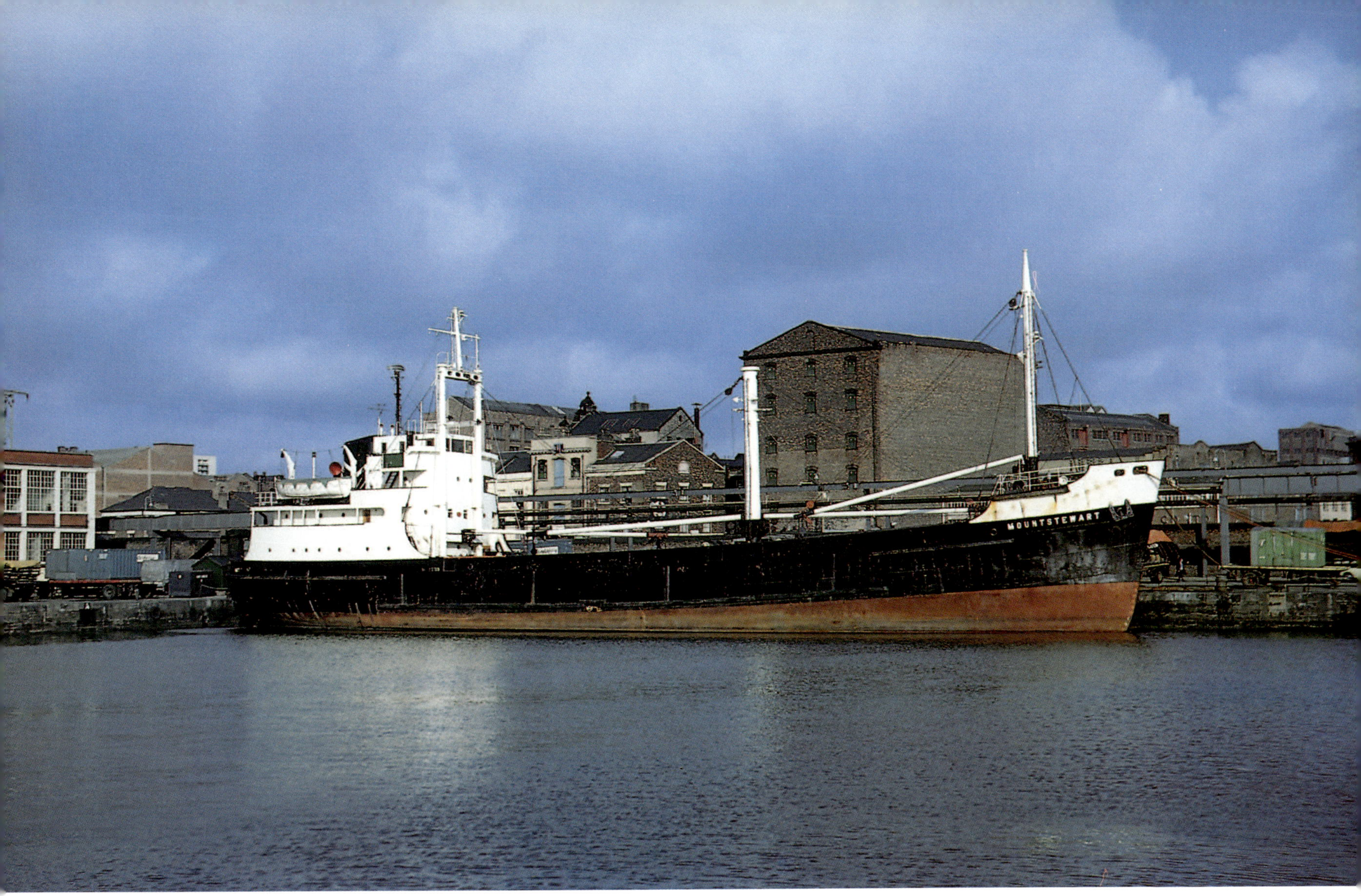

The ***Mountstewart*** (892grt/55) is seen at Berth 36 in Trafalgar Branch Dock during early Autumn 1968 and almost at the end of her career with Coast Lines. She was built at Ardrossan as ***Essex Coast*** for Coast Lines and was renamed ***Mountstewart*** following transfer to the Belfast, Mersey and Manchester Company in 1957. In 1960, she was placed under the ownership of the Belfast Steam Ship Company but reverted to Coast Lines ownership in 1965. Bought by Greek owners in 1968, she became ***Evdelos***, later taking the names ***Michalis*** in 1972, ***Proodos*** in 1976 and ***Manuel*** in 1979. She was eventually scrapped at Salamis in 1986.

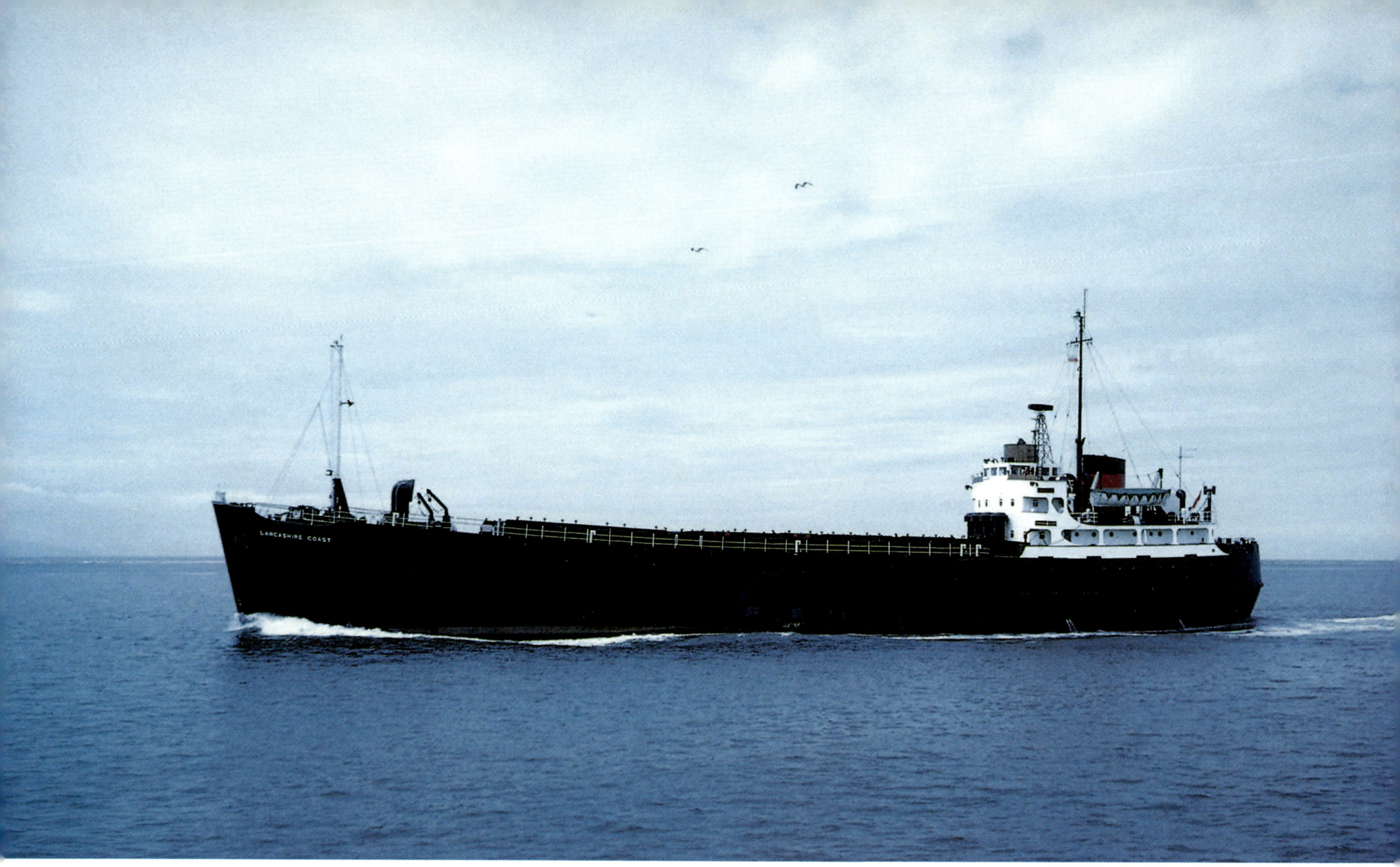

The coasters of Coast Lines with their black funnels and white chevrons, along with associated companies of Coast Lines, were long associated with the port of Liverpool and we have two of the company's vessels on these pages. Firstly, we see the ***Lancashire Coast*** (1283grt/54) in the Mersey during the Summer of 1972. She was built by Charles Hill & Sons Ltd in Bristol and was launched on 18 November 1953, being handed over to the Belfast Steamship Co. Ltd in April of the following year. This was an associated company of Coast Lines and its ships had a red funnel with black top as seen here. She was renamed ***Trojan Prince*** briefly in 1968 when chartered by Prince Line for its Mediterranean service, resuming her original identity in 1969. She survived long enough to be converted for the carriage of containers and was subsumed within the P&O Ferries fleet in which she retained her name. She was sold to Mediterranean operators in 1980 and was converted to a livestock carrier named ***Paolino***. She was eventually demolished at Salamis in the Spring of 1984. Some sources say she was scrapped at Chalkis.

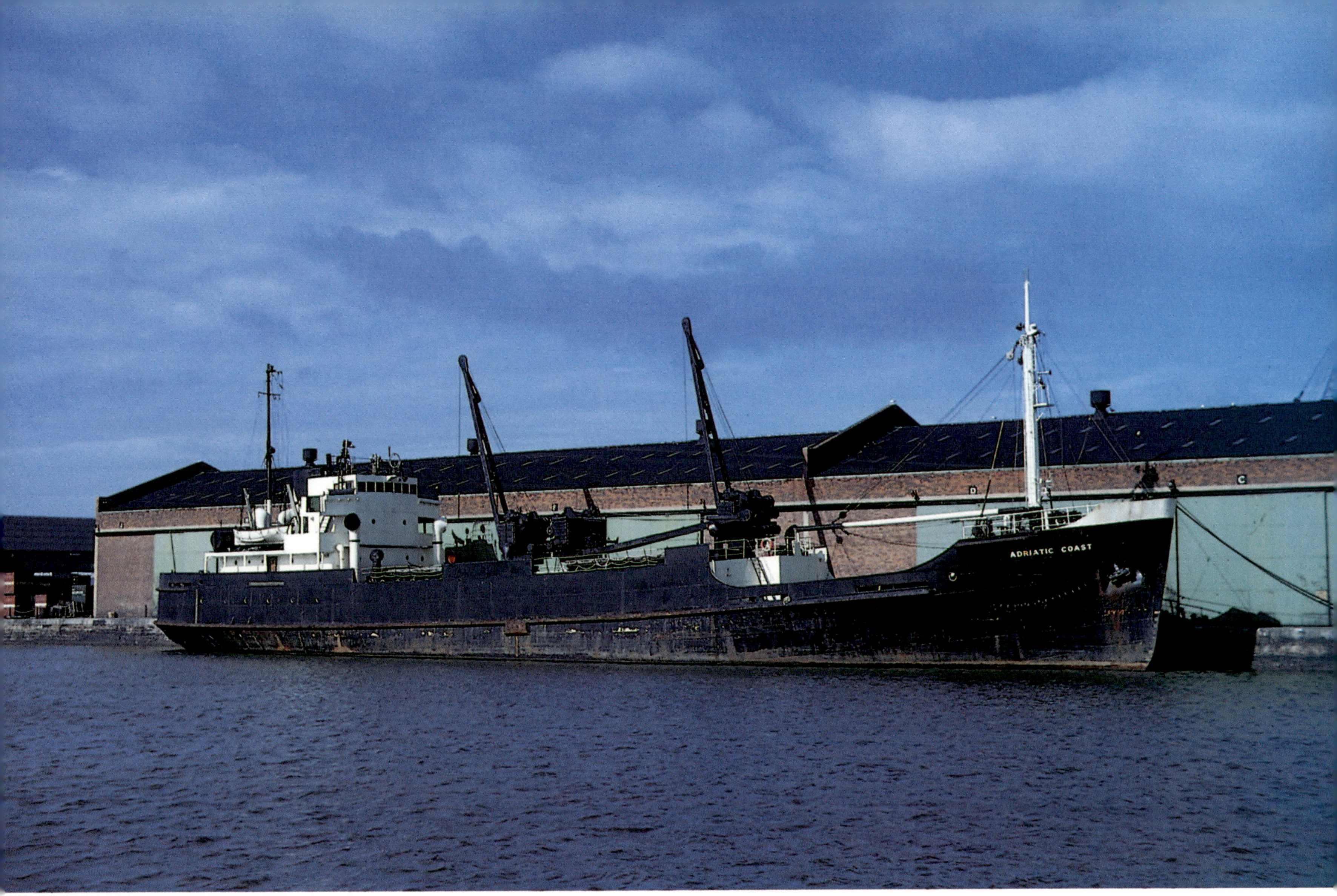

Our second Coast Lines vessel is older. The ***Adriatic Coast*** (1050grt/49) was a product of the Hall, Russell shipyard in Aberdeen. She was launched on 1 March 1949 and completed in May 1949. Like many similar vessels of her generation, she found a ready buyer in the Mediterranean after almost two decades in service with the Coast Lines group and she was renamed ***Trader*** in 1968, later becoming ***Ermis*** in 1972, ***Potamia*** in 1973 and finally ***Stella III*** in 1975. As such, she was broken up in 1980. She was photographed in early Autumn 1968, with sale imminent.

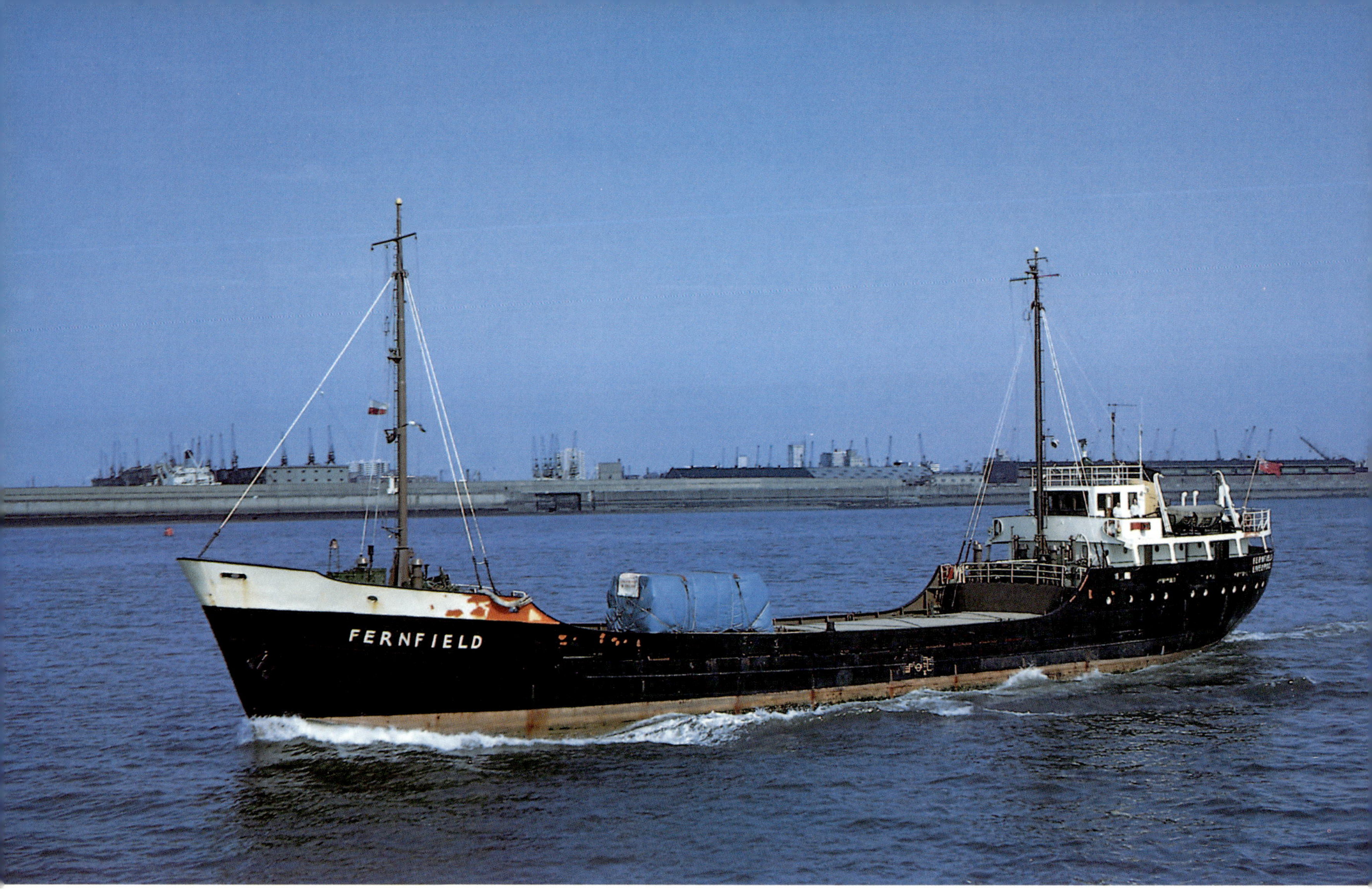

The ***Fernfield*** (561grt/54) sails out of the river with a single item of deck cargo in Summer 1970. Built at the Waterhuizen shipyard of Gebr van Diepen, her keel was laid as ***Huybergen*** but she was launched as ***Haaksbergen*** on 25 September 1954, being handed over to her Dutch owners two months later. She joined the Zillah Shipping fleet in September 1958. In 1965, she was chartered by Anglo Irish Transport Ltd, a subsidiary of Coast Lines, and was converted to carry unit loads, working mainly from Preston to Londonderry and Portrush. She was transferred to Coast Lines ownership when this company took over Zillah on 31 December 1967. In 1971, she was sold to James Tyrrell, of Arklow, and was renamed ***Shevrell***. The following year she was sold to Canadian operators by whom she was renamed ***Coudres De L'Ile***. She sank on the 15 June 1988 following a collision in the St.Lawrence off Pointe au Boisvert.

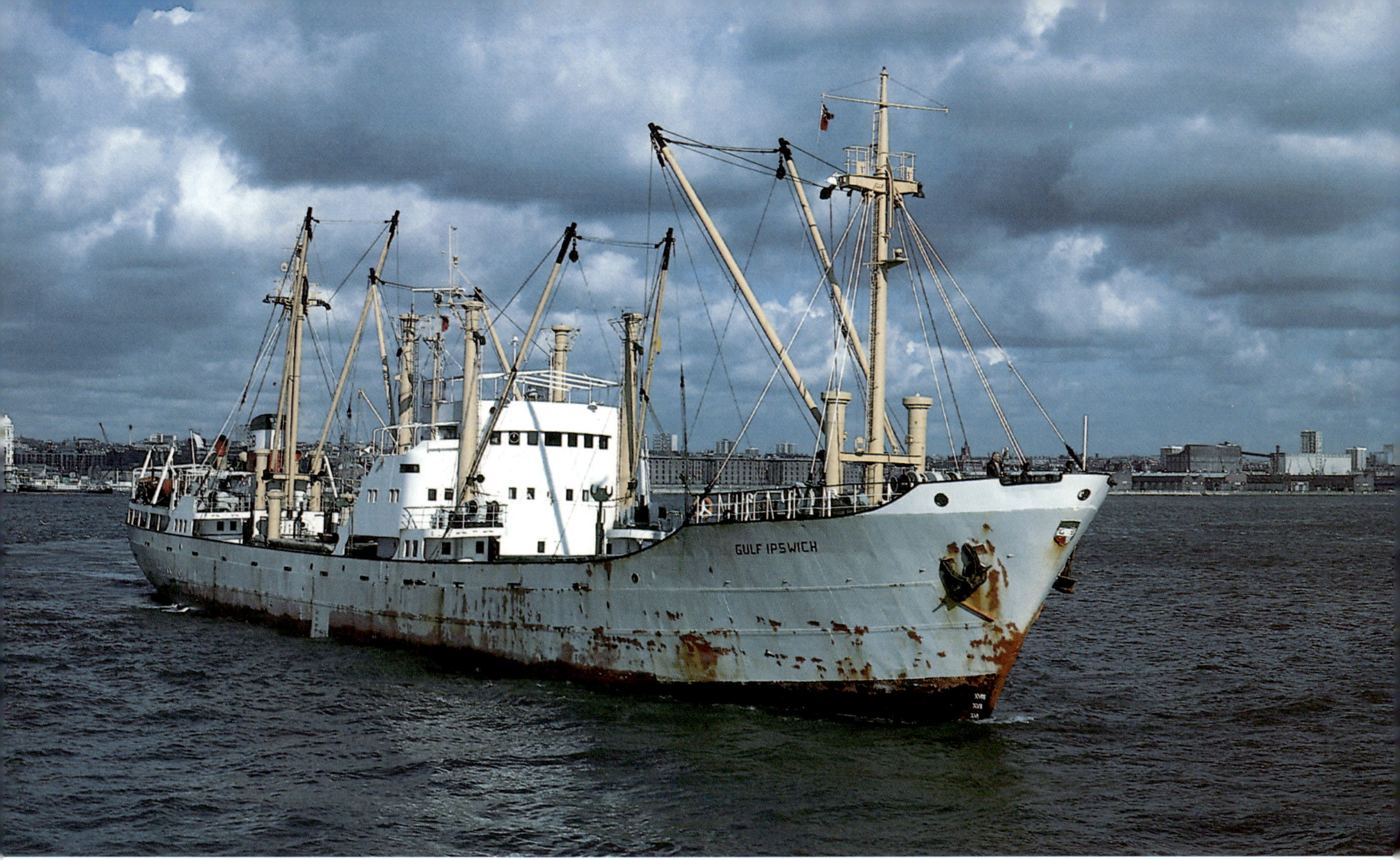

With a classic bridge-amidships profile, the ***Gulf Ipswich*** (CYP, 1373grt/57) approaches the Alfred lock entrance on 20 July 1976. She was the fifth vessel to enter the fleet of the Gulf Maritime Co Ltd, a company established in 1971 and with an operational base in Ipswich. She was built at the Nobiskrug shipyard in Rendsburg as ***Helga Russ*** and launched on 27 May 1957. In 1970, she was acquired by Spliethoff's and renamed ***Leidsegracht***, becoming ***Gulf Ipswich*** when entering the Gulf Maritime fleet in 1973. Although remaining with this company, she was renamed ***Moon*** and then ***Ashanti*** in 1977. On 18 November 1981, she collided with the ***Carina*** (GRC, 41914grt/67) off the Hook of Holland when outward bound from Dordrecht to Ipswich. She proceeded to Ipswich for repairs prior to re-entering service. On 5 April 1983, she was laid up in the River Blackwater, eventually leaving on 10 September of that year following sale to Dutch breakers. She arrived at Zwijndrecht on 8 October, and demolition was completed on 16 January 1984.

(C J Tabarin)

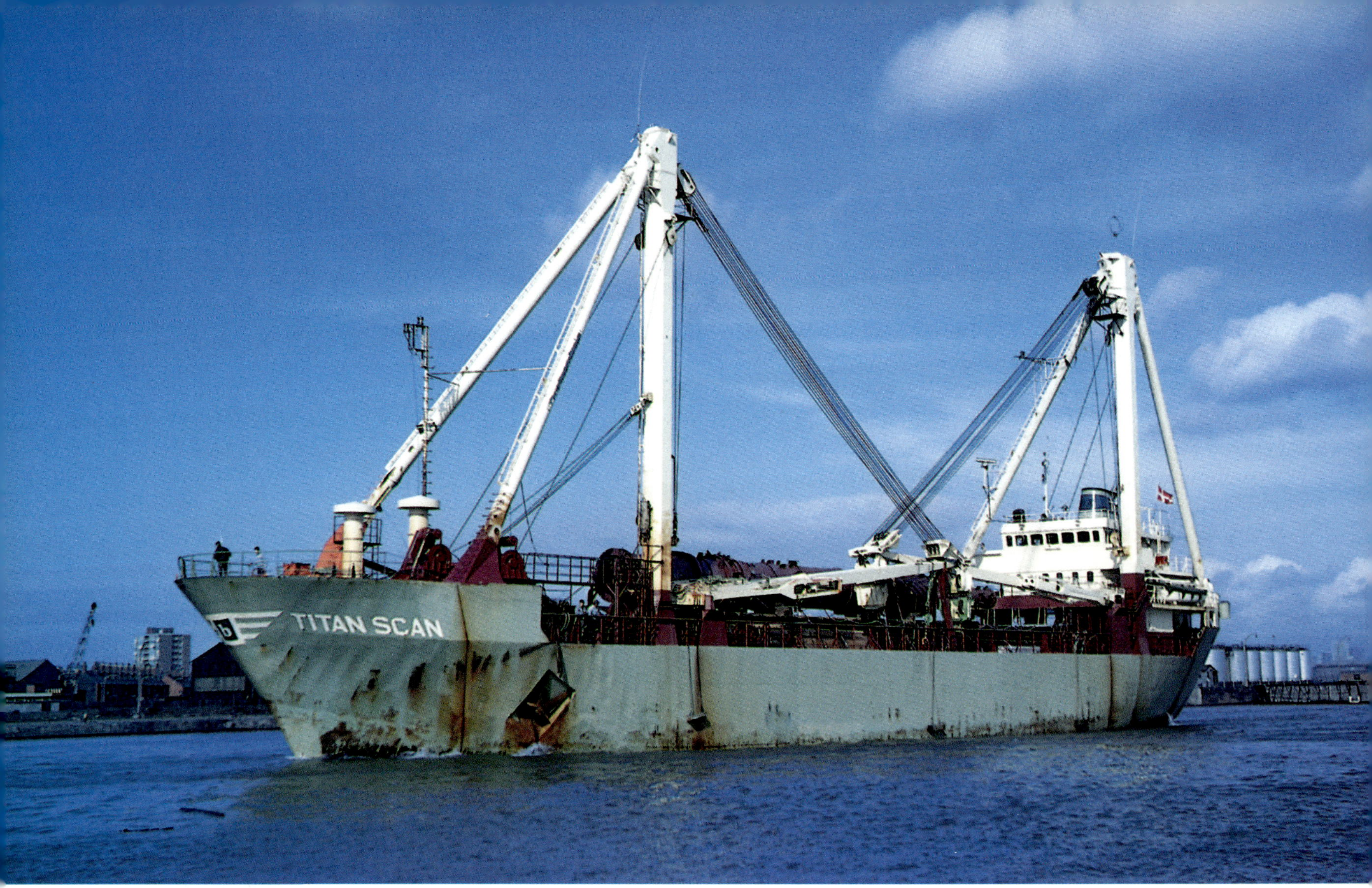

Photographed in Spring 1972, the huge derricks on the ***Titan Scan*** (DNK, 1317gt/70) mark her out immediately as a ship built for the carriage of heavy lifts. Each derrick had a 95-ton lift capacity. Built by Sønderborg Skibsværft, she was launched on 29 August 1969 and handed over to her original Danish owners on 20 February 1970. In 1979, she was sold to Panamanian-flag operators and renamed ***Biscayne Star*** and then became ***Molunat*** in 1982 following sale to Atlanska Plovidba. In 1994, she was sold on to a Singapore investment company and leased to Karumba Shipping, an Australian company. She was rebuilt as a livestock carrier and continues to trade as such in mid-2007.

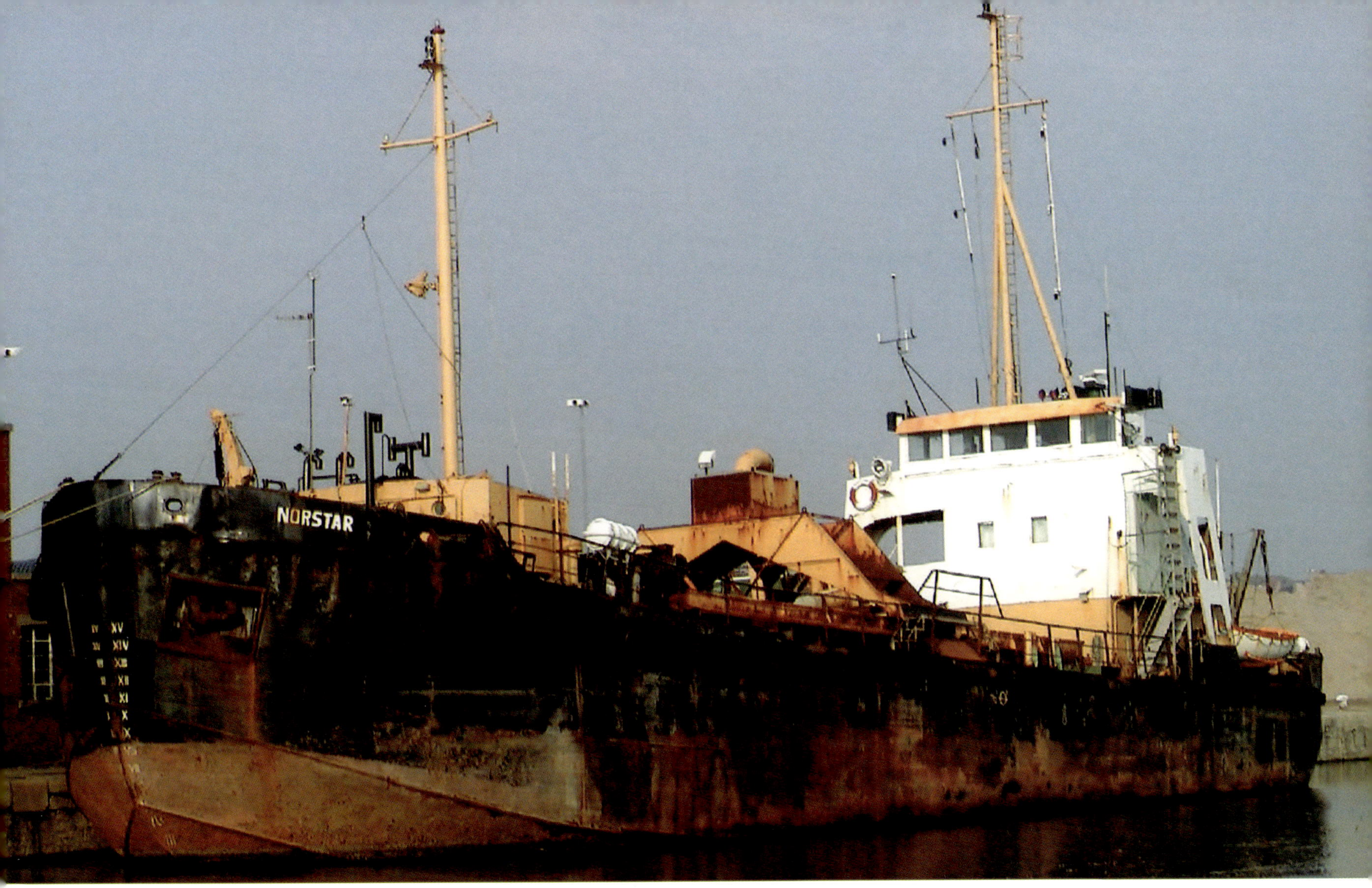

The ***Norstar*** (614grt/61) was built at the Bristol shipyard of Charles Hill & Sons Ltd for Norwest Sand and Gravel Company and operated as a sand dredger in the River Mersey. This company was established in the early 1950s when the long-established Bristol-based T R Brown and Sons sought to expand its business beyond the Bristol Channel. Initially, two small dredgers were transferred from the Bristol Channel, but the ***Norstar*** was the second of three dredgers built specifically for use on the Mersey. She was launched on 8 December 1960 and was powered by a Ruston & Hornsby engine. When the Brown family bought Alexander McNeil & Co Ltd, of Greenock, along with dredging rights in the Clyde area in 1966, the ***Norstar*** was moved to the Clyde. She was sold for demolition in 2002 but was not broken up at Liverpool until 2005.

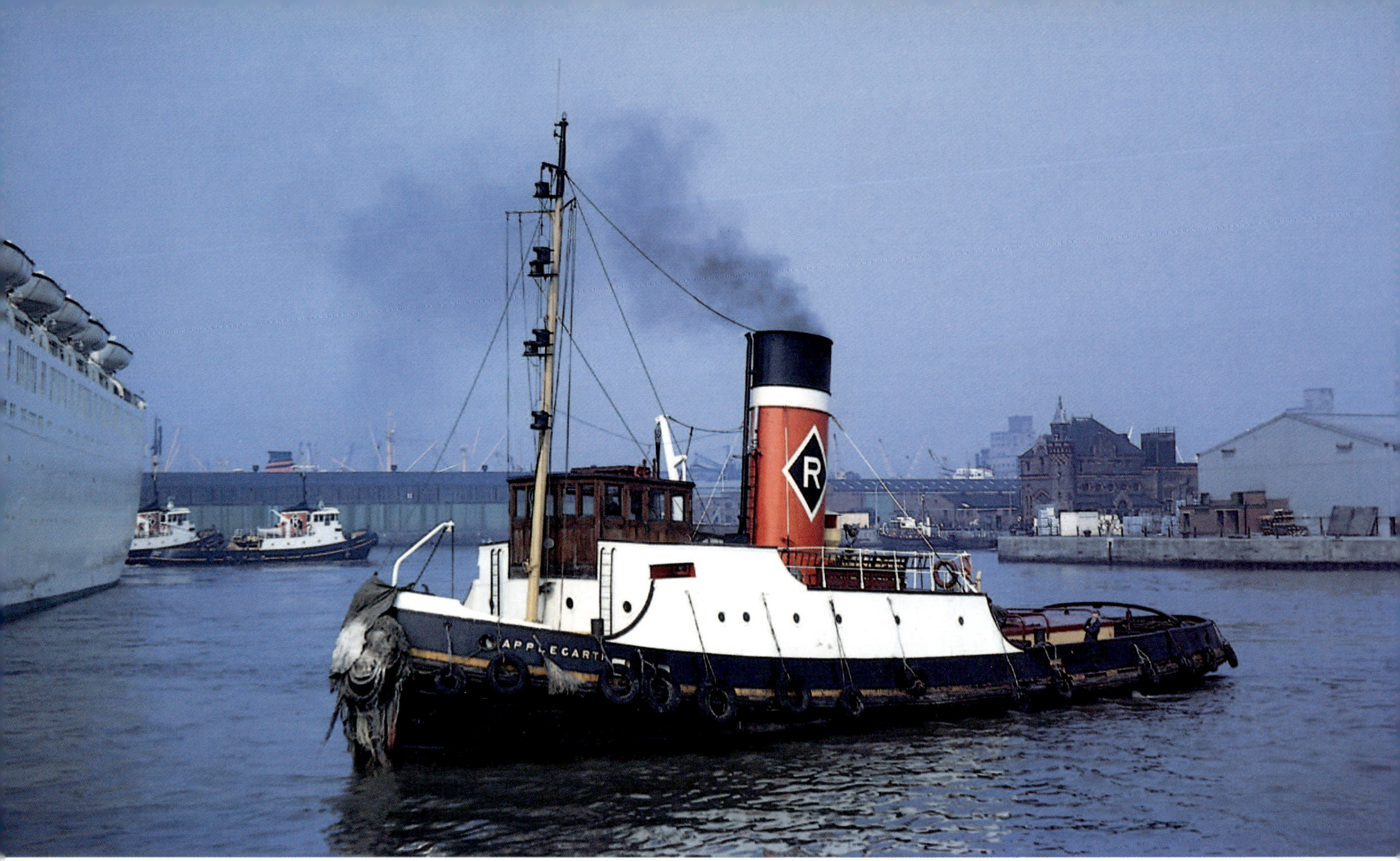

The ***Applegarth*** (231grt/51) was one of a series of similar tugs that worked on the river in the 1950s and 1960s. She was built at Aberdeen by A Hall & Co Ltd for the Rea Towing Company and was launched on 28 December 1951. Handed over on 24 April 1951, she was to have an eventful career. She represented the Rea company in the Mersey Pageants of Shipping held in July and August 1951 to mark the Festival of Britain celebrations in Liverpool. Three displays were held and the tugs, ferry steamers, Dock Board craft, Liverpool Corporation ships and the North Wales steamers took part. On 19 August 1954, she sank in Liverpool's Canning Dock following overhaul and was raised three days later. Converted to burn fuel oil in September 1956, the next noteworthy incident was tragic. When assisting the ***Perthshire*** on 13 January 1960, she sank with the loss of her entire crew. She was raised on 28 January, repaired and returned to service some six months later. Sold to Holyhead Towing Ltd, she became ***Afon Cefni*** in 1971. She left the UK two years later when bought by Greek owners and renamed ***Achilles***. A further sale within Greece saw her become ***Vernicos Christina*** in 1975 and she was broken up at Perama in October 1980.

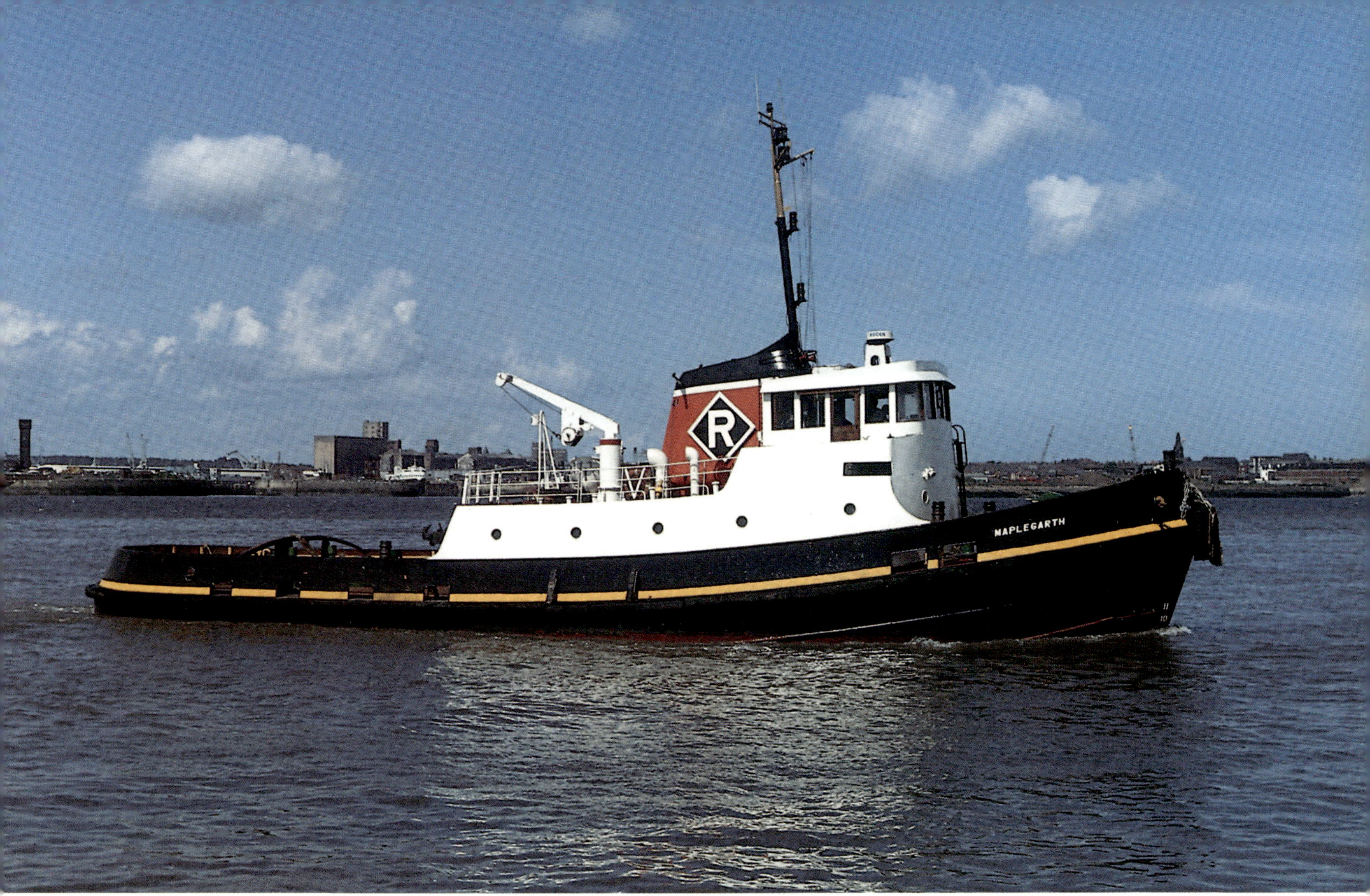

Photographed in June 1984, the ***Maplegarth*** (213grt/62) was one of a pair of tugs of hydroconic hull design built for Rea Towing at the yard of P K Harris & Sons Ltd in Appledore. Launched on 22 September 1961, she was handed over to her owners on 7 March of the following year. In 1985, the Rea company was taken over by Cory Ship Towage Ltd, soon to become simply Cory Towage Ltd. She left the Mersey in September 1992 when sold to a Falmouth company by whom she was renamed ***Seagarth***. She was driven by two 4-stroke 6-cylinder Ruston & Hornsby diesel engines with a total output of 1300bhp and geared to a fixed-pitch propeller. Many have considered her design to be one of the finest for any motor tug.

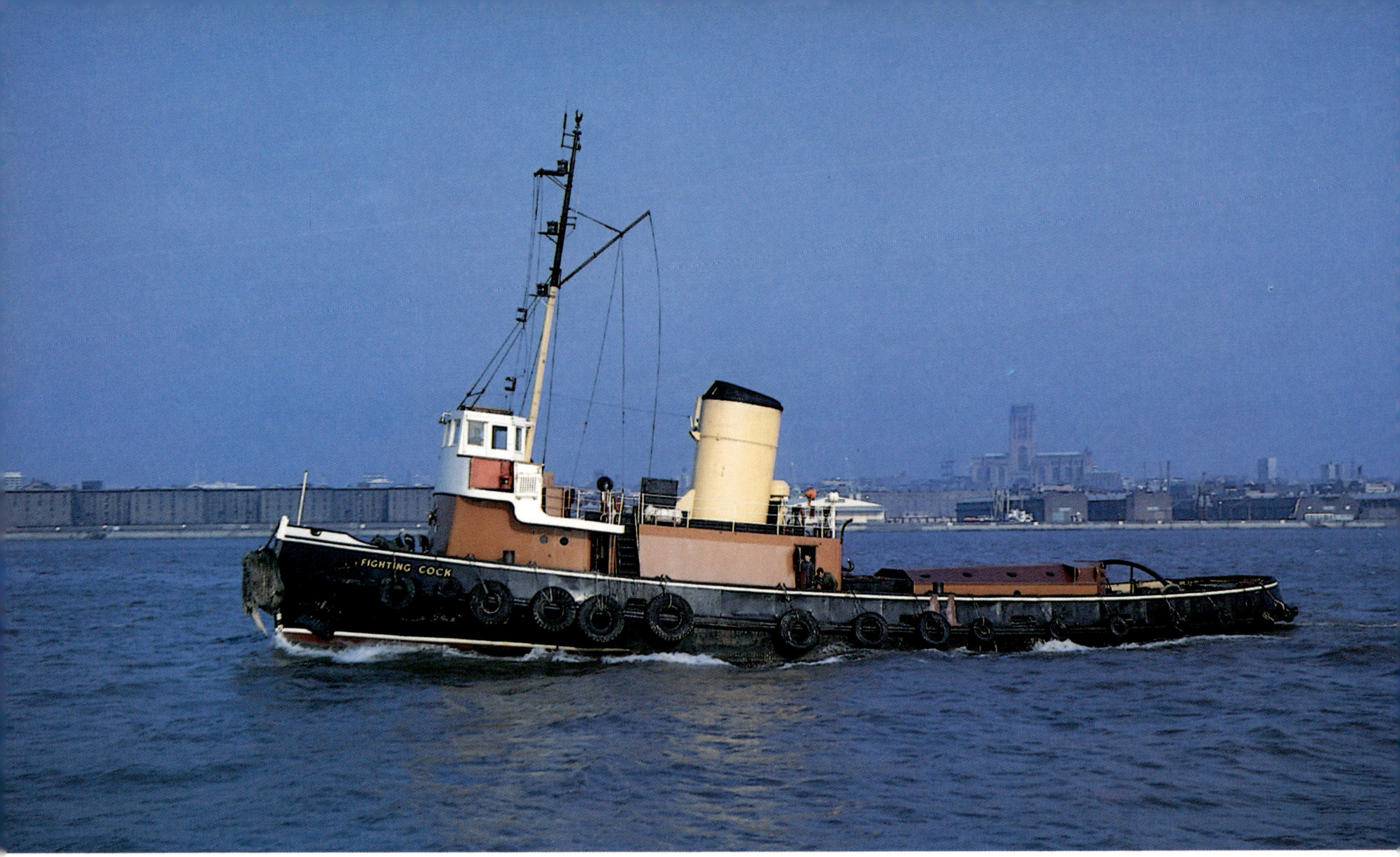

The ***Fighting Cock*** (218grt/53) is seen off Cammell Laird's south yard. Of considerable historical interest, she was one of a pair of tugs built locally by Cammell Laird and both launched on the same day, 12 May 1953. The second tug in the fleet to bear this name, she and her sister tug ***Game Cock V*** were the first two tugs to be owned by North West Tugs Ltd which was operated and managed by the Liverpool Screw Towing Company. They were used to move the aircraft carrier ***Ark Royal*** from the Cammell Laird shipyard to drydock in 1954 and again assisted her from the Mersey when she was commissioned in February 1955. The ***Fighting Cock*** was adopted by a squadron of the Royal Air Force and presented with a replica of the squadron's crest - a fighting cock. Together with the ***Game Cock V***, she was partly rebuilt in 1960, being given a shorter funnel and adapted to burn fuel oil. The Liverpool Screw Towing Company was taken over by the Alexandra Towing Company in December 1966 but the ***Fighting Cock*** was not renamed until the autumn of 1970 when she became ***Sloyne***. Exactly one year later, she was sold to a Greek operator and was renamed ***Vernicos Nicos***, sistership ***Game Cock V*** becoming ***Vernicos Costas***. The ***Vernicos Nicos*** was scrapped in 1988.

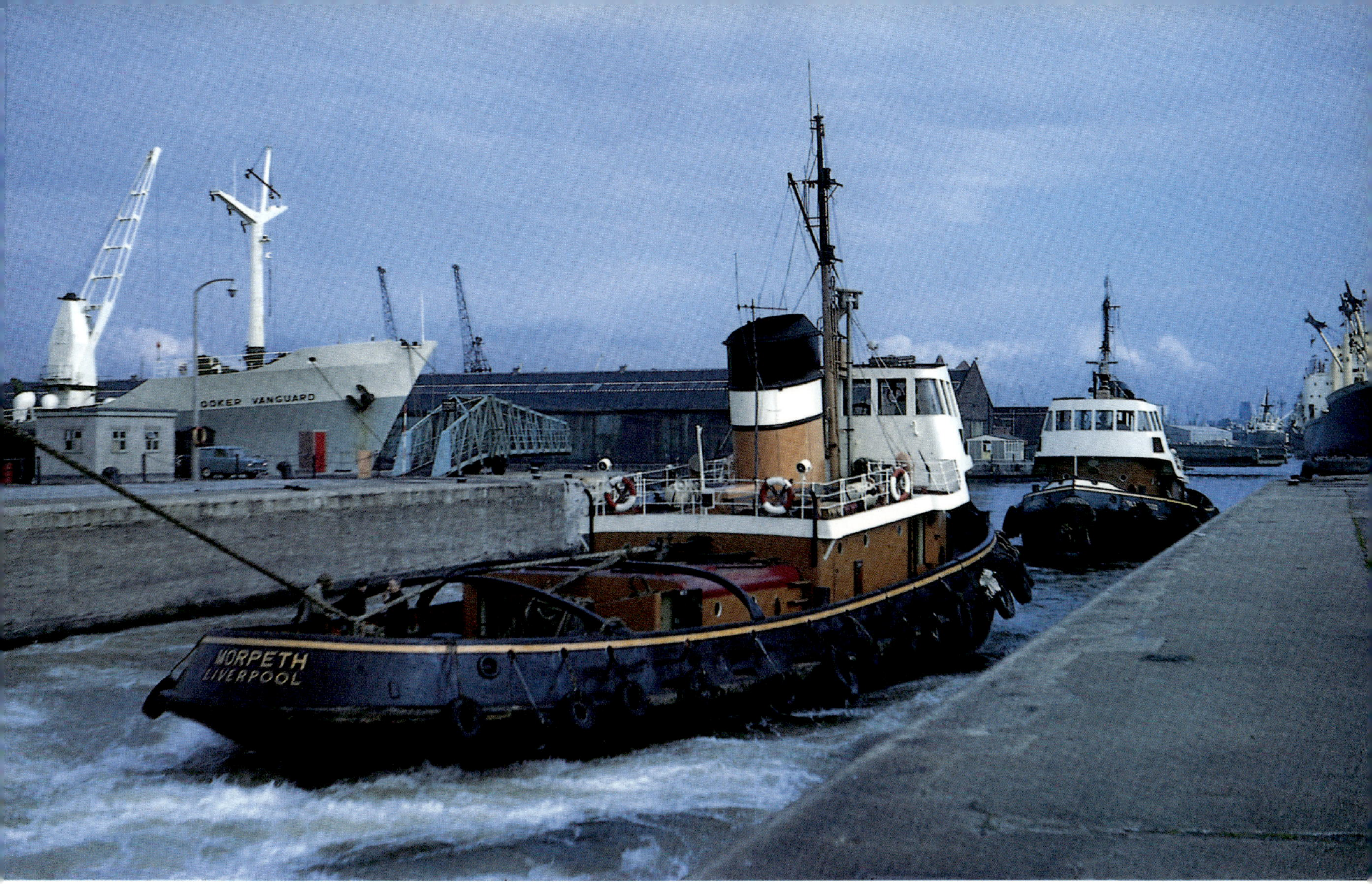

The ***Morpeth*** (193grt/58) also began life as part of the North West Tugs fleet. She was one of a pair of tugs ordered by parent company Liverpool Screw Towing from the Cammell Laird yard in Birkenhead. No ordinary tugs, these two were to be the first motor tugs built specifically for use on the Mersey. This tug, then named ***West Cock***, was the second of the pair and was launched in early March 1958. She joined the Alexandra fleet in 1966 and was renamed ***Morpeth*** in 1970. She left the Mersey bound for Greece in 1981, becoming another purchase by the Vernicos Shipping Company who renamed her ***Vernicos Giannis***. On 9 August 1983, she sank off Iraklion (Heraklion) after colliding with the ***Atalante*** (GRC, 12614grt/63). She was refloated on 20 October and taken in tow but she broke adrift in bad weather eight days later and sank off Falconera in the Cyclades.

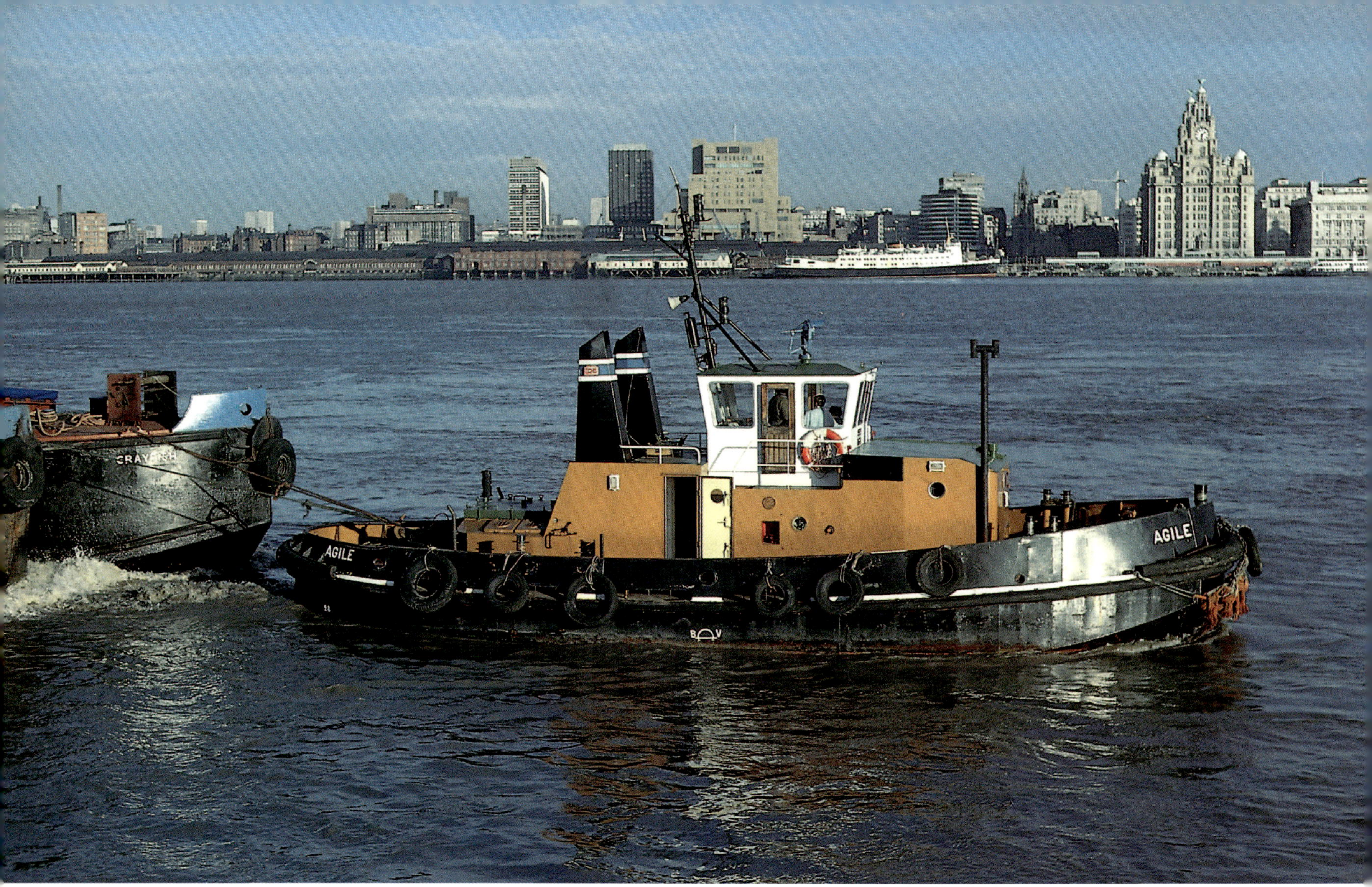

A rather unexpected addition to the Mersey towage scene in 1978 was the small tug ***Agile*** (51grt/71). She was built by Ziegler Freres at Dunkerque and worked at this French port for the first three years of her life before moving on to Boulogne for the next four years. In 1978, she was acquired by Bulk Cargo Handling Services, a newly-established company within the Alexandra Towing Co Ltd group, and was to be used for towing barges in the Mersey. It is this role which she is fulfilling in this photograph as she approaches the Alfred Lock entrance in January 1981. After a decade on the Mersey, she was transferred to the Alexandra fleet on the Thames. In 1994, with Alexandra now part of the Howard Smith group, she joined the latter's fleet on the Humber and was eventually sold to operators in Waterford in 1997. There she was usually used for harbour maintenance work while being offered for re-sale.

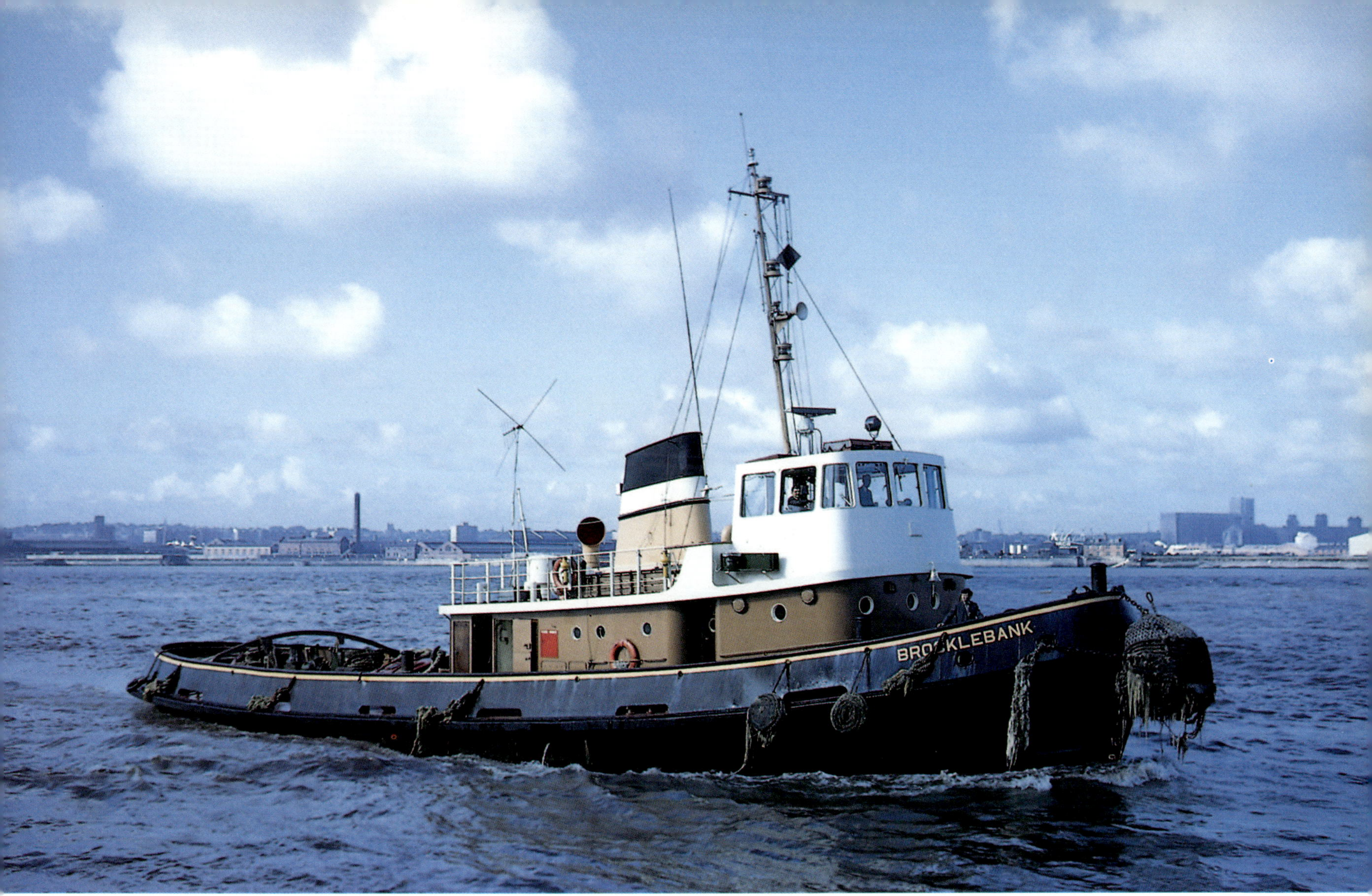

The Alexandra Towing Co Ltd's tug ***Brocklebank*** (173grt/64) on service in the River Mersey in 1968. The ***Brocklebank*** was built in 1965 at the Northwich yard of W J Yarwood and launched on 28 August 1964. She was part of an order for six tugs placed by her owners, three being allocated to the Yarwood yard and destined for Alexandra's fleet in Southampton, and the other three to the Hessle shipyard of Richard Dunston Ltd. The latter three were for the Mersey fleet. These vessels incorporated all the latest techniques in tug design and equipment. The ***Brocklebank*** is now preserved at the Merseyside Maritime Museum at Albert Dock in Liverpool but remains in working order and visits various maritime festivals throughout the year.

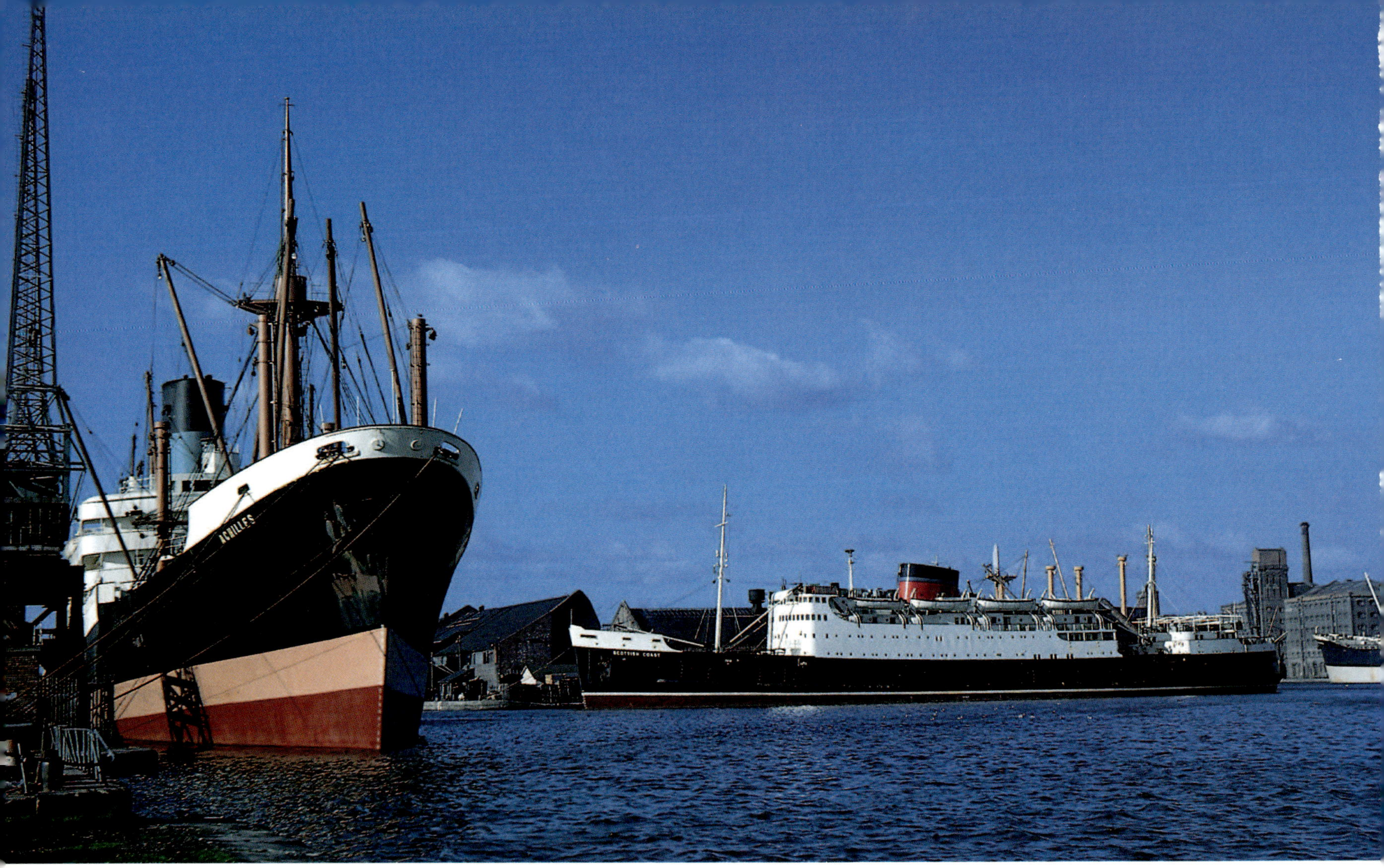

The ***Scottish Coast*** (3817grt/57) is seen in the East Float at Vittoria Wharf in Birkenhead in late 1968 as her name is about to be changed to ***Galaxias*** following sale by Coast Lines to Greece. She was launched at the Harland & Wolff shipyard in Belfast on 21 August 1956 and completed on 1 March 1957. Unlike the ***Irish Coast*** which she displaced from the Glasgow - Dublin route in August 1957 (see page 58), she never had a Coast Lines funnel although the chevron was outlined in rivets on that funnel. From the summer of 1965 onwards, she operated out of Ardrossan, a hoist being placed in the forward deck to allow side loading of up to 25 cars, but relieved other vessels in the winter when they were off service for annual overhaul. She became ***Princesa Amorosa*** in 1989 and was beached for demolition at Mumbai on 24 December 2002. To complete the scene, we see Blue Funnel's ***Achilles*** (7875grt/57). Built at the Vickers-Armstrong shipyard on Tyneside, she was launched on 13 May 1957 and handed over in October. Between May 1972 and April 1973, she was renamed ***Dardanus*** and was the sold to Chinese owners and renamed ***Kaigo***. She was scrapped in Calcutta where she arrived on 5 June 1982.